The Canadian
HERITAGE
Celebration of
Mothers

The Canadian HERITAGE Celebration of Mothers

Edna McCann

Prentice Hall Canada Inc.
Scarborough, Ontario

Director of Trade Publishing: Robert Harris
Production Editor: Mary Ann McCutcheon
Copy Editor: Kelli Howey
Assistant Editor: Joan Whitman
Production Coordinator: Julie Preston
Cover Design: Julia Hall
Cover Image: Tony Stone Images/Ron Krisel
Page Layout: BJ Weckerle

1 2 3 4 5   F   02 01 00 99 98

Printed and bound in Canada

Literary Credits

Photo Credits

Visit the Prentice Hall Canada Web site! Send us your comments, browse our catalogues,
and more. **www.phcanada.com**.

Thank you, Mommy, I love you.

Edna

Introduction

While writing *The Canadian Heritage Celebration of Mothers* I have been reminded of all the blessings my life has given me. I have been both a daughter and a mother. I am now a grandmother. All three of these roles have filled my days with meaning and happiness.

As mothers we are born again in the eyes of our children, and we live our lives over through them. We are able to share their joys and their defeats, their sorrows and their triumphs and that experience, the unpredictable voyage of mother and child, is magical. We are buoyed along this journey by our commitment to mothering well. To love is the ultimate goal of all mothers. Most remarkable is when mothers embark on the journey of raising their children without expectation or condition, without guarantee that their efforts will be appreciated and rewarded. And it is that leap of faith, that complete and utter lack of expectation, that makes the miracle.

My gratitude goes out to all my readers, in a way a part of my family, for they believe in me the way a mother believes in a child, with a conviction that is strong and unwavering, ever present and sustaining.

Edna McCann

A Mother's Prayer

Father in Heaven, make me wise,
So that my gaze may never meet
A question in my children's eyes;
God keep me always kind and sweet,

And patient, too, before their need,
Let each vexation know its place,
Let gentleness be all my creed,
Let laughter live upon my face!

A mother's day is very long,
There are so many things to do!
But never let me lose my song
Before the hardest day is through.

Margaret Sangster

The joy of being a mother, grandmother, and great-grandmother may hardly be adequately described in words. I cannot imagine what my life would be like without my children.

At one time or another, my children have made me feel happy, sad, proud, anxious, cheerful, angry, peaceful, annoyed, enchanted, thrilled, heavy-hearted, overjoyed, ecstatic, jubilant, and gratified.

The delightful thing about having children is that you never know from one day to the next which of these many adjectives is going to best describe you.

Most of us stumble into motherhood in a blissfully ignorant state, assuming, with the exuberance of youth, that we are able to handle anything that comes our way.

As our children grow up, and we ourselves become more mature, it becomes obvious that being a mother probably isn't as easy as we originally thought.

When we try to deal with teenagers, boyfriends, girlfriends, and the emotional roller coaster that is a part of raising young adults, we may occasionally question our original decision to have children at all. Then, suddenly—overnight—they are adults, embarking on their own lives and leaving us to wonder where the years went.

Then we are given grandchildren and we see again the wonder, the joy, and our connection to the ages.

A mother's love is unique, unconditional. Uncompromising and never-ending.

In her book, *Motherhood, The Second Oldest Profession*, Erma Bombeck wrote, "I was one of the luckier women, who came to motherhood with some experience. I owned a Yorkshire terrier for three years."

In my case, I came to motherhood with tremendous confidence and enthusiasm. After all, hadn't I played with dolls from the time I could toddle? Hadn't I helped out in the church nursery every Sunday? How much more difficult could it be to have a baby of your own?

This feeling of assurance and well-being lasted until the first time that Mary, our firstborn, had been fed, changed, and placed lovingly in her beautifully decorated bassinet—where she proceeded to scream with all of the fervour and volume that her little lungs could produce. I believe that she was about twenty-four hours old. From that time, until she was nearly three months old, it became a contest to see which of us could cry more.

For some reason, a number of babies come into this world happy and contented, eating, sleeping, smiling on cue—crying only when factors such as hunger or a wet diaper warrant. Others, such as Mary, arrive in a frenzy of unhappiness; usually, as we know, a result of colic. The only comforts that seemed to calm this girl were a hot water bottle on her tummy and constant motion. Night after night, my husband, George, would warm the hot water bottle, place it on his shoulder and, somehow, place Mary such that he was able to secure her with one arm. Thus he was able to keep her moving while he retained one arm free to write a sentence or two of his sermon as he passed his desk with each circuit of the study. Eventually, Mary would fall asleep for a few hours before her wailing would waken me and it would be my turn to walk.

Thankfully, in the daytime, both George's mother and my mother would take Mary for walks in her carriage—where, if she was crying, the sound was somewhat muffled by the blankets and the carriage hood.

This was not my idea of what motherhood was going to be.

I loved this wee soul with every fibre of my being, but being unable to comfort her was an enormous frustration for us all.

And then one day, Mary stopped crying. On that day (which I still remember as one of the happiest of my life) it was as if someone had flipped a switch. Gone was the miserable little soul and in her place was the baby I had been expecting all along. Gone, as well, was the perpetual knot in my stomach, and my joy and happiness were unrestrained.

A baby is God's opinion that life should go on.

Carl Sandburg

My mother was the making of me. She was so true and so sure of me. I felt that I had something to live for, someone I must not disappoint. The memory of my mother will always be a blessing to me.

Thomas Alva Edison

With the tremendous advancements in science and technology, tiny babies who, years ago, would have been at extreme risk for survival, are now not merely surviving, but thriving and enjoying completely normal lives.

I'm sure that almost all of us know of someone whose baby has spent time in the neonatal specialty area of a hospital, attached to machines that monitor heart rate, breathing, weight gain or loss, while maintaining a constant temperature; it's easy to see how these tiny babies are being given every chance.

Now try to imagine, if you can, having one of those wee mites with none of the help that is available now. This is just what happened to Lillian Milne, a very dear friend of my mother's, back in 1914.

Lillian and Bert, her husband, were looking forward to the birth of their first child. Picture their surprise and panic when Lillian went into labour nearly two months early.

It was not a difficult labour, but when their daughter was born, she was very tiny—weighing just two pounds—and she was not breathing. Thankfully, the doctor, in desperation, used a technique not yet in vogue—blowing directly into the baby's mouth—and shortly thereafter the tiny girl began to breathe on her own.

However, she was not out of the woods yet! Knowing that it was important to keep her warm, her parents placed her bassinet in the kitchen beside the stove. Although it was the month of May, Bert, Lillian, and their many relatives kept the stove going day and night to keep the baby's temperature stable.

Over the next few weeks, her condition went up and down, but as she began to gain weight, she seemed to get stronger with each passing day.

Does this story have a happy ending? Indeed it does! Alberta and her two younger sisters, Marion and Mildred, continue to be three of my dearest friends. Alberta was a miracle baby in 1914, and although her survival was in jeopardy, her longevity attests to the "never give up" attitudes of her family and their doctor.

God could not be everywhere, that is why he made mothers.

Hebrew saying

The thing about having a baby is that thereafter you have it.

Jean Kerr

Three special words the world holds dear—"Mother," "Home," and "Love."

A mother who walks with God knows He only asks her to take care of the possible and trusts Him with the impossible.

Ruth Bell Graham

The recent use of fertility drugs has allowed multiple births to become much more commonplace. Today, twins, triplets, quadruplets, and even quintuplets are born with great frequency.

This was not the case back in 1934 when, in the small town of Callander, Ontario, the Dionne quintuplets were born. Their birth was called the "obstetrical event of the century," and their combined weight (measured on a potato scale!) was a mere thirteen pounds, six ounces. The tiny girls— Yvonne, Annette, Cecile, Emilie and Marie—born to their French-Canadian parents Oliva and Elzire Dionne, were wrapped in blankets and placed in two baskets that were kept warm with heated bricks and flatirons. They stayed in these makeshift incubators until real incubators could be rushed to the remote farmhouse. Their struggle for survival continued for months under the supervision of Dr. Allan Roy Dafoe, the doctor who helped to deliver the babies.

During their first year, the babies, in spite of their parents' protests, were made wards of the Crown, and a board of guardians was set up to administer their affairs.

What happened over the next five years is really quite tragic. Reared behind high fences, guarded by police, and exhibited in a glassed-in playground, these adorable girls drew visitors to the small town of Callander at the rate of five thousand to six thousand people a day. The girls had endorsement contracts that earned them a collective fortune of nearly a million dollars, but they remained separated from their parents. It was not a happy time in their lives. Naturally shy and inhibited, the girls found it difficult to be constantly watched. One day, when one of the sisters was holding up a monkey-faced doll to the large audience, Annette was heard to say, "Put it down or they shall think we are six!"

Oliva and Elzire battled in court for eight years before the girls were eventually restored to them, and the entire family (including the couple's other five children) were able to live together under one roof.

The Dionnes are the only identical quintuplets known to have survived to adulthood, although Emilie died at age 20 during an epileptic seizure, and Marie passed away in 1970, after a brief illness.

The real tragedy is that we know the separation of the girls from their parents had a lasting traumatic effect on them. Although the nurses were kind to them, nothing could take the place of their parents' nurturing.

At the time it all seemed quite reasonable, as the quintuplets were a "never before seen" phenomenon. Today, this separation would be unheard of—and for that we may all be grateful.

A mother is one who can take the place of all others, but whose place no one else can take.

There is only one pretty child in the world, and every mother has it.

Chinese proverb

A mother's love perceives no impossibilities.

Who of us is mature enough for offspring before the offspring themselves arrive? The value of marriage is not that adults produce children, but that children produce adults.

P. DeVries

I was a young bride and a young mother. When you are young, you assume several things:
You are invincible
You are immortal
Your baby will be born healthy
I have been lucky in all three of those beliefs. So far, I am invincible; I remain immortal (although I seem to be becoming more mortal by the day); and my babies were all born healthy.

My good friend, Mary O'Donnell, shared those same assumptions until the birth of her fifth child. When the doctor told Mary that her newborn son was a "Mongoloid" (at that time this was the word used to describe a baby affected by Down's syndrome) and should be institutionalized, she felt as if her world were falling apart.

Back in those days, children who were "retarded," or physically handicapped, were routinely placed in special homes or institutions and their parents were encouraged to forget about them and "get on with their lives."

Mary asked to see her son and, against the advice of the nurses, the doctor—and even Johnny, her husband—announced that her son would be coming home.

It was not an easy time. David (or "Peanut," as the family called him) had difficulty nursing and each feeding took hours. With the demands of the rest of the family to be dealt with, Mary became more and more tired and discouraged. She said, "I was nearly ready to give up when something wonderful began to happen. Johnny started to take an interest in his wee son. Always a champion of the underdog, he set about helping with Peanut's feeding—crooning, humming, and then laughing with delight when Peanut finished a whole bottle. The children, as well, began to see that although it would take longer, with their help Peanut could learn to do things. It was also an asset that he was the happiest and most contented child on earth. Just seeing a brother or sister would bring a huge smile to his face. It was the children who taught Peanut to roll over and to sit up, endlessly propping him up with cushions and pillows until eventually he was able to sit alone.

"Peanut went everywhere with us, no babysitters for him. He came to the rink to watch his brothers play hockey. He came shopping with us, to church, and to Brownie and Cub Scout meetings. Other people began to see what a delightfully happy child he was and how much his family adored him.

"It was not always easy, though. When a new child in the neighbourhood had the temerity to yell 'Your brother's retarded,' John Jr. got into the first—and only—fistfight of his life. Some people stared or made unkind remarks. Instead of being embarrassed, it made the other children fiercely protective of him.

"Like many other children with Down's syndrome, Peanut had heart problems that would require surgery. We took him to the hospital on a day as sunny as his disposition. We couldn't know that he would not be coming home again. The operation was more difficult than even the eminent heart surgeon imagined, and Peanut didn't make it through the operation. He was just eight years old when he died, but in those short years, he accomplished a lot. He gave us a firm understanding of fortitude and perseverance. He was the glue that bonded his siblings together to protect him. He was lovable and he was loved."

Today, we know that many children with severe mental or physical handicaps can lead happy and productive lives. I like to think that Mary, Peanut, and their family led the way to at least some of the understanding that we now have.

"Isn't there one child you really love the most?" a mother was asked. She replied, "Yes. The one who is sick, until he is well; the one who is away, until he is home."

Anonymous

How cherished the home where the family is valued, and everyone knows he belongs.

Life is a flame that is always burning itself out, but it catches fire again every time a child is born.

George Bernard Shaw

One laugh of a child will make the holiest day more sacred still.

Robert Ingersoll

A mother's children are portraits of herself.

Who takes the child by the hand, takes the mother by the heart.

Danish proverb

My thanks to the unknown author of these lovely lines.

COME IN FOR A MOMENT

You're always welcome at my house,
Come in and hang your hat;
The tea is brewing on the stove,
We'll sit and have a chat.

But if you can't look past the clutter
Or ignore the dusty floor,
You'll want to come another day
To call here at my door.

For yesterday my broom and dustpan
Never left their spot;
My dishes still lie in the sink
With dirty pans and pots.

You see, my children needed me
To share some joys and fears,
To bounce them gently on my knee
And wipe away their tears.

CELEBRATION OF MOTHERS

So last upon my busy list
Was sweeping up the dust,
For someday they'll no longer need
A mother's tender touch.

You're always welcome at my house
Come in and hang your hat;
Just remember love comes first
And housework's always last.

*Maternal love is a miraculous substance which
God multiplies as He divides it.*

Victor Hugo

Our old family doctor, Don Gorton, once told me, "You will never know how your children have turned out until your grandchildren are grown." I have to say that my children have turned out very well and this is confirmed by the fact that I have wonderful grandchildren. I'm sure that my husband, George, were he alive today, would have been so proud.

I often think that mothers can learn some things by watching their children. When my own children were young, I was constantly amazed by their simplicity and tireless energy. If we could retain some of these qualities as we grow older, I'm sure that we would be happier people.

Happy are those who live in the dream of their own existence, and see all things in the light of their own minds; who walk by faith and hope; to whom the guiding star of youth still shines from afar, and into whom the spirit of the world has not entered.

William Hazlitt

One of the loveliest of all services in the Christian church is the service of baptism. As the daughter and the wife of ministers, there was nothing more joyful for me than bringing our own children to be embraced into the faith that was so much a part of our lives. Mary, Margaret, and Julia were each baptized in a different church (as ministers were moved frequently in those days), but each service was performed by our closest friend, Roland Hill. Rolie and George had graduated together and each had committed to the other that they would baptize the other's children—no matter where, no matter when. It was a commitment honoured by each.

I think what I liked best about Rolie was his complete understanding of children. When we had Julia's christening service, Mary and Margaret were of the age of curiosity but with little patience for sitting quietly for any length of time.

The service simply wasn't moving along quickly enough to suit them and they began looking for things to do. They wandered up to peer into the baptismal font, after which they chose to join the organist on the bench. Rolie didn't bat an eye, nor did he break stride in his service except to say, "Girls, I think Uncle Rolie has some pennies for treats," whereupon he put his hand into his pocket and dropped all of his change (which was considerable) onto the floor. The girls spent the rest of the service picking up their "treasures" and Rolie baptized baby Julia in relative peace and calm.

A happy family is but an earlier heaven.

Sir John Bowring

L ast summer, during a stay with my dear friend Eleanor in Muskoka, I was delighted to be included in a family gathering for a christening service. The service was held in the beautiful old Anglican church in Beaumaris, on Lake Muskoka. The children being baptized were Maxwell and Frances deGruy, grandchildren of my friends Nancy and Henry Armstrong. For me, this gathering was a testament to the rich family history that is so much a part of Muskoka.

Both Henry and Nancy are American, from the Pittsburgh area of Pennsylvania. Their families were some of the first cottagers in the area, and Henry,

Nancy, and their brothers and sisters and cousins spent many happy summers enjoying all that the region has to offer.

The years passed, and the families grew and found work in areas all across the United States. Each summer all would return to Muskoka for a holiday that would reunite the sons, daughters, cousins, and their many new offspring.

As Nancy told me, "It is here, in Canada, that our families have spent many of our happiest moments together. It is here that we really get to know one another. Playing golf or tennis, swimming and boating, having sleepovers, barbecues, birthday parties, or just sitting on the dock talking, gives us a chance to appreciate each other. It also gives our children and grandchildren a wonderful sense of the family history as they see pictures of many generations of us on the cottage walls or in the numerous photo albums in each cottage."

Nancy and Henry's daughter, Mimi, and her husband, Mike, were proud parents as their children were baptized in the church where they themselves had been married a few years earlier.

The small church was filled with many friends and family members and it brought tears of joy to my eyes as I realized what a wonderful and special relationship exists for these dear friends of mine.

Years from now, Max and Frances will be able to walk into this church and see their names in gold on the wooden baptismal plaques beside so many others and know that they are a part of a happy loving family with special roots in Muskoka and Canada.

What will your children remember? Moments spent listening, talking, playing and sharing together may be the most important times of all.

Gloria Gaither

Many have forgotten the value and the meaning of traditions. They are the characteristics and activities which identify a family as unique and different.

Dr. James Dobson

"A smile happens in a flash, but the memory of it can last a lifetime." There is probably nothing that is more memorable than a baby's first smile. As a mother, I remember each of my daughters' first "real" smiles (not to be confused with the little grins that come with gas!). Because Mary was such an unhappy child, I probably watched even more intently than most new mothers to see any indication that my baby might smile. It came after a particularly frustrating day, when it seemed that no amount of rocking, walking, or pushing her in her carriage would bring her relief. Finally, exhausted, I sat down in the wing chair and just laid her on my arm. Suddenly, she looked up at me and smiled, a big face-lighting smile. I, of course, immediately began to cry. George, who was sitting at his desk, turned just in time to see the end of her smile and his wife in tears again. I can still close my eyes and see that smile, and today it brings a smile to my face as well.

Thankfully, Margaret was a much happier baby and I am still certain that her first smile came when she was only a few weeks old. Mary and I were peeping into the bassinet when she opened her eyes, looked right at Mary, and smiled. Mary was thrilled and could hardly wait to tell anyone who would listen that baby Margaret's first smile was just for her. I truly believe that Marg's first smile was the beginning of the close friendship that has existed between them for all of their lives.

Julia, our youngest daughter, has always had a flair for the dramatic, and she loves an audience. She saved her first smile for a propitious moment during a meeting at the church, when the committee was about to vote on authorizing funds for some much-needed repairs to the manse, our home.

I was bringing tea and cookies to serve at the meeting, so I asked George to hold Julia for me.

"Gentlemen," said George, "I would like to introduce my daughter, Julia."

She looked right at the committee, and smiled. It was a wonderful smile that simply shone forth in the room. The men were delighted and even the most dour of the group seemed pleased to have had Julia's smile bestowed upon him.

I like to think that it was Julia's smile that helped influence the committee to approve the funding for the restoration of our home.

The memories of those first smiles really do last a lifetime.

Joy is not in things, it is in us.

Richard Wagner

Of all the joys that lighten suffering earth,
what joy is welcomed like a newborn child?

Caroline Norton

Some of my earliest memories of my own childhood are of sitting on my mother's knee while she read to me. We had an enormous wooden rocking chair with several large cushions placed for comfort. It would take almost no coaxing from me—mother would drop whatever she was doing if I asked her to read to me. I am sure that I developed my great love for books because of my mother's willingness to share endlessly of her time to read (and re-read) my favourite books.

Clarence Day, a well-known American author, wrote of his own memories of bedtime stories.

"When we boys were very little, we used to go to mother's room Sunday evenings, on our way upstairs to bed, and sit in a circle around her. She told us a story from the Bible or talked to us about how good we ought to be and how much we ought to love God. She loved God herself as much as she dared to, and she deeply loved us, and she was especially tender and dear on those Sunday evenings. One of my brothers told me years afterward how much they had meant to him in those days, and how he had cherished the memory of them all his life."

The mother's heart is the child's schoolroom.

Henry Ward Beecher

I enjoyed these words from an unknown author. I hope you will take pleasure from them as well.

WHAT MAKES A HOME

A man can build a mansion
Anywhere this world about,
A man can build a palace
Richly furnish it throughout,

CELEBRATION OF MOTHERS

A man can build a mansion
Or a tiny cottage fair,
But it's not the hallowed place called "Home,"
'Til Mother's dwelling there.

A man can build a mansion
With a high and spacious dome,
But no man in this world can build
That precious thing called "Home."

A man can build a mansion
Carting treasures o'er the foam,
Yes a man can build the building
But a woman makes it "Home."

*Home is the place where character is built,
where sacrifices to contribute to the happiness
of others are made, and where love has taken
up its abode.*

Elijah Kellogg

*Though motherhood is the most important of
all professions—requiring more knowledge
than any other department in human affairs—
there was no preparation for this office.*

Elizabeth Cady Stanton

Many years ago, when I was having children, there really was very little written that might be helpful to a new mother. We were totally dependent upon information (and mis-information) from members of our family or friends, and of course the family doctor in the case of illness.

And then came Dr. Spock. Dr. Benjamin Spock, M.D., practised pediatrics in New York City from 1933 to 1947. He then became a medical teacher and researcher at the Mayo Clinic, the University of Pittsburgh, and the Western Reserve University in Cleveland. Although he wrote eleven books, *Dr. Spock's Baby and Child Care*, first published in 1946, became a bible for generations of mothers. This book has been translated into thirty-nine languages and has sold more than forty million copies worldwide.

The first edition of the book took three years to write, with the doctor dictating and his wife, Jane, typing the original draft of the manuscript long into the night. As well, Jane was responsible for such details as how many diapers, nighties, or bottles to recommend. She also tested various ways to prepare formulas to be sure that they worked.

It was also Jane who held consultations with specialists and publishers, and who spent hundreds of hours doing last-minute revisions and indexing.

The most wonderful thing about this book was that it seemed to provide answers for nearly every possible question that a new mother (or father) could ask.

My daughter, Marg, and her husband, Bruce, used *Dr. Spock's Baby and Child Care* religiously when they were raising their children, Phyllis and Marshall. Although they added their own common sense to rearing their children, Marg felt that the book gave her a sense of confidence that she might not otherwise have had.

In the introduction of the book, a letter to the reader explained well how to use the book. It said, in part, "Your doctor knows your child and is therefore the only person in a position to advise you wisely. . . . This book is not meant to be used for diagnosis or treatment; it is only meant to give you a general understanding of children, their troubles, and their needs. . . . Every child is different, every parent is different, every illness or behaviour problem is somewhat different from every other. . . . Remember that you are more familiar with your child's temperament and patterns than I would ever be."

Youth fades, love droops, the leaves of friendship fall: a mother's secret hope outlives them all.

Oliver Wendell Holmes

If you want your children to turn out well, spend twice as much time with them and half as much money.

Dear Abby

Your child will never grow too old to hear you say "I love you."

Dr. Jan Dargatz

Romance fails us—and so do friendships—but the relationship of Mother and Child remains indelible and indestructible: the strongest bond on earth.

Theodor Reik

The family is one of nature's masterpieces.

George Santayana

Sometimes, when we least expect it, being a mother becomes a difficult and painful experience. I was thinking today of Jill Kelly, whose son was born with Krabbes disease, a degenerative neurological disorder that would slowly decrease his hearing, his sight, and all of his mental faculties—and that would, ultimately, at a very early age, prove fatal.

Until February of 1997, the Kelly family seemed to have it all. Jim Kelly was the outstanding quarterback of the Buffalo Bills, in the National Football League. During his eleven years in the league he had led the Bills to four consecutive appearances in the Super Bowl, the NFL's championship game. Jim earned a high salary and invested well, and in January of 1997 he retired from football to spend time with his wife, Jill, their daughter, Erin, and their baby, expected in February.

Baby Hunter James was born on Valentine's Day, February 14, a wonderful thirty-seventh birthday gift for father Jim.

Hunter was very irritable, but the Kellys put it down to adjusting to new surroundings or colic. It was not until the Kellys took Hunter to the doctor for an ear infection that they learned of a possible problem. The doctor felt that Hunter was exhibiting signs of cerebral palsy. A visit to a neurologist at the Children's Hospital in Buffalo eliminated that diagnosis and came up with the heartbreaking discovery that Hunter had Krabbes disease, one of the group of illnesses known as leukodystrophies. Extremely rare, occurring in only about forty people in the United States each year, it is a genetic disease that gives the infantile sufferer a life expectancy of about only thirteen months.

Shortly after Hunter's diagnosis, doctors implanted a tube in his stomach because he had lost his swallowing reflex. As well, he was given anti-seizure and anti-reflux medication. Jim prepared the formula before Jill fed him, and then, in the evenings after his feeding, Jill would take him into their Jacuzzi bath, which seemed to relax him. Hunter often fell asleep in the tub, cradled in his mother's arms.

What can you possibly do when your son has been given a death sentence? The Kellys chose to love him and give him as much care as possible—with Jill spending twenty-four hours a day with him. Jim spoke candidly about his wife. "People say that I am tough, but I could never do what Jill does. Her patience and motherly instincts are unmatched. Her strength amazes me."

In September of 1997, Jim and Jill established "Hunter's Hope," a foundation that they hope will heighten awareness about Krabbes disease and raise funds to assist in research—and hopefully to find a cure. The Kellys hope that by helping others they will have given some meaning to their son's brief life.

Most of all, the other beautiful things in life come by twos or threes, by dozens and by hundreds. Plenty of roses, stars, sunsets, rainbows, brothers and sisters, aunts and cousins, but only one mother in the whole world.

Kate Douglas Wiggin

CELEBRATION OF MOTHERS

A mother's love is what makes a house a home; it's what makes a family a family.

If you bungle raising your children, I don't think whatever you do well matters very much.

Jacqueline Kennedy Onassis

Babies are nature's way of showing people what the world looks like at 2 a.m.

The finest inheritance you can give to a child is to allow her to make her own way, completely on her own feet.

Isadora Duncan

We have not completely fulfilled our responsibility as parents until we bequeath to our children a love of books, a thirst for knowledge, an awareness of beauty, an understanding of loyalty, a vision of greatness, and a good name.

William Arthur Ward

Every mother is like Moses. She does not enter the promised land. She prepares a world she will not see.

Pope Paul VI

Never fear spoiling children by making them too happy. Happiness is the atmosphere in which all good affections grow.

One of my greatest fears as a mother was that my children, who were very picky eaters, would develop rickets or scurvy or some other dread disease of the malnourished—and it would be all my fault.

I tried everything that I could think of to introduce a variety of foods into the girls' diet, but it was no use. They ate only what they wanted and spit out the rest.

Apparently, I worried needlessly, because my daughters have grown up to be healthy women, who eat well and who will try any culinary dish offered them.

I was interested to learn that experiments have been done to find out exactly what children would eat, given a variety of wholesome foods and left to their own desires.

From one such experiment, it was discovered that babies who chose their own diet from a variety of nutritious (unrefined) foods developed very well, becoming neither too fat nor too thin. As well, over time a baby chose what any doctor would agree was a well-balanced diet.

However, from meal to meal and day to day, the appetite varied and each individual meal was not necessarily balanced. A baby would sometimes eat nothing but applesauce or perhaps days of only cereal, but eventually their choices provided the well-balanced, doctor-recommended, healthy diet.

These findings likely explain, then, why my great-grandson, Justin, lived through his first three years and is, today, a strapping teenager and a big strong football player.

My granddaughter, Phyllis, then a new mother of twins, probably worried more than most about her children's diet because of their low birth weights. Her concern for their healthy development caused her to worry endlessly about what Justin and Jenny ate.

Jenny was a "good" eater, happily taking in whatever was offered and enjoying every mouthful. But for three years, Justin ate an unvaried diet of Cheerios with milk, peanut butter sandwiches, Kraft macaroni and cheese dinner, and cauliflower. He couldn't even be persuaded to eat a hamburger or french fries.

As a mother, married to a doctor, and conscious of what constitutes a balanced diet, Phyllis tried everything she could think of. Eventually, however, she just gave up and let Justin eat his self-restricted diet.

"I felt like a terrible mother, but when I gave up worrying I saw that he seemed to know on his own when to add something new to his diet."

As young mothers, we worry about everything to do with our children. Apparently diet is one item that can be moved down the list of worry priorities.

My daughter, Margaret, printed this lovely poem for me when she was in primary school. It made that Mother's Day one that I cherish to this day.

We can only have one mother,
Patient, kind and true,
No other friend in all the world,
Will be so true to you;
For all her loving kindness,
She asks nothing in return;
If all the world deserts you,
To your mother you can turn.

We can only have one mother,
No one else can take her place;
You can't tell how much you'll need her,
'Til you miss her loving face.

Be careful how you answer her,
Choose every word you say,
Remember she's your mother,
Tho' now she's old and grey.

We can only have one mother,
Oh, take her to your heart.
You cannot tell how soon the time,
When you and she must part.
Let her know you love her dearly,
Cheer and comfort her each day,
You can never get another,
When she has passed away.

Years ago, it was uncommon for women to work outside the home, and as a result, mothers usually became excellent cooks—if only because they had infinite practice. It seemed that "mothering" and "cooking" were synonymous in many ways.

Of course there are exceptions to every rule, and my daughter's best friend's mother was one of these exceptions. Enid's cooking was, to be blunt, dreadful! My daughter told me of her memories of Enid's meals. "Mom, I can remember sitting down at Karen's house and not even recognizing anything that was being served.

"The funniest thing was that no matter how awful it was, we always enjoyed it when Karen's dad would say, 'Enid, you've done it again, another delicious meal.' How could we kids ever disagree with her father? Not only that, but her mom always took time to tell us how she had added a 'dash' of this and a 'pinch' of that just to make it 'special.' I honestly began to question my own taste buds because by the time we finished eating, Enid would be fairly glowing from the family's praise.

"Then one day at school, our teacher asked if we could bring cookies for a bake sale to be held to raise funds for a class trip. On the day we were to bring the cookies, I met Karen on the way to school. I came up behind her and was surprised to see her emptying the cookies into the ditch beside the road. She gave me a guilty smile when she saw me.

" 'Don't tell!' she made me promise. When I had agreed, she went on. 'You know that my mom's a dreadful cook, so I made cookies that look the same to substitute for hers.'

"For heaven's sake, Karen, I thought you all loved your mom's cooking. Every time I eat at your house, you all rave about the meal. How come?'

" 'That's easy,' she replied, 'We love her.' "

A mother is a person who, seeing there are only four pieces of pie for five people, promptly announces that she never did care for pie.

CELEBRATION OF MOTHERS

The phrase "working mother" is redundant.

Jane Sellman

If a child is to keep alive his inborn sense of wonder, without any such gift from the fairies, he needs the companionship of at least one adult who can share it, rediscovering with him the joy, excitement, and mystery of the world we live in.

Rachel Carson

For me, motherhood has been the one true, great and wholly successful romance. It is the only love I have known that is expansive and that could have stretched to contain, with equal passion, more than one object.

Irma Kurtz

I actually remember feeling delight at two o'clock in the morning, when the baby woke for his feeding, because I also longed to have another look at him.

Margaret Drabble

There is an enduring tenderness in the love of a mother to a son that transcends all other affections of the heart! It is neither to be chilled by selfishness, nor daunted by danger, nor weakened by worthlessness, nor stifled by ingratitude. She will sacrifice every comfort to his convenience; she will surrender every pleasure to his enjoyment; she will glory in his fame, and will exult in his prosperity—and, if misfortune overtake him, he will be dearer to her from misfortune; and if disgrace settle upon his name, she will still love and cherish him in spite of his disgrace; and if all the world beside cast him off, she will be all the world to him

Washington Irving

A mother understands what her child does not say.

Jewish proverb

The successful mother sets her children free and becomes more free herself in the process.

Robert J. Havighurst

Once you are a mother, you are always a mother. This fact is perfectly illustrated in this little story about Eleanor Roosevelt and her son, James.

At a dinner honouring his mother, James, then in his early fifties, was seated on the dais next to her. After coffee, James rose to speak. He began by saying he was grateful for the opportunity to sit down for dinner with his much-travelled and very busy mother. Then he confided that he had just been overwhelmed by memories, for during the main course his mother had leaned over and ordered, in a whisper, "James, eat your peas."

My mother gave me this recipe and it is one that I have passed on to my daughter and my grandchildren.

"Take a half-dozen children, two small dogs, a pinch of clear, rippling stream, and some pebbles. Pour the ingredients in a large grassy field, stirring constantly. Pour the brook over the pebbles, sprinkle the field with wild flowers, spread a deep blue sky over all and bake in a hot sun. When the children are all well-browned, remove and set to cool in a bathtub."

As a young mother I waited, with eager anticipation, to hear my daughters' first words. I spent many hours with my face pressed close to theirs murmuring "Mama, Mama." They would smile, blow bubbles and make unintelligible sounds. I would lean into the carriage saying "Mama"; I said "Mama" as I changed their diapers and "Mama" as I fed them.

And then one day, they would each smile sweetly and say "Dada." The first word that came out of all three girls was "Dada." I probably should have been upset after all the hard work but, in fact, I found it quite humorous. I also found it to be quite restful, as they would wake up in the night saying "Dada." George could never resist the call and I would roll over and at least pretend to sleep.

For some mothers, a child's first word may be even more special. A mother in Scotland, whose little girl was handicapped, wrote a poem to celebrate her daughter's first word. The mother's thrill and wonder after months of love, prayer, and hope are evident in her lines.

> Today she spoke her first short word
> Nothing in that you say
> But it's something I have asked for
> When every night I pray.

CELEBRATION OF MOTHERS

She's one of many children
Less fortunate than some,
But oh to me she's wonderful
Today my child said "Mum."

*I remember my mother's prayers; they have
clung to me all my life.*

Abraham Lincoln

*Children do not know how their mother loves
them until they have children of their own.*

*Mother—in this consists the glory and the
most precious ornament of woman.*

Plato

*My point is, that no matter what the ordinary
person says . . . no matter who it is that speaks,
or what superlatives are employed, no baby is
admired sufficiently to please the mother.*

E. V. Lucas

*Every child born into the world is a new
thought of God, an ever-fresh and radiant
possibility.*

Not flesh of my flesh
Nor bone of my bone,
But still miraculously my own.
Never forget for a single minute,
You didn't grow under my heart,
But in it.

When I read those lines, I think of Gail, a dear friend of my daughter, Margaret. Gail and her husband, John, were married for a number of years, and during that time they waited expectantly for Gail to become pregnant. Well-meaning family members and friends would ask over and over when the young couple would be starting a family.

"I longed to have a baby, and their questions would hurt so much. Eventually we decided that adoption might be the right choice for us. We went through an agency with all of the paperwork, questions, home visits, and waiting that is involved in finding a child.

"Finally, we received the call we had been waiting for: 'Mrs. McCarthy, we have a baby for you. It's a boy!'

"I had been collecting baby things for months, we had decorated a room, and I was ready to be a mother—until that phone call. Suddenly I was filled with self-doubt. I was panicky and I found myself breathing so fast that I was hyper-ventilating and feeling faint. I called John at work and I could scarcely speak. When I heard John say 'Thank you, God,' I was able to pull myself together.

"When the agency lady placed our baby son in my arms, I was transformed. I was a mother! No matter that he was not of my body, he was mine— every one of his tiny fingers and his peach-fuzz hair were mine. He made us a family."

That was many years ago, and now John and Gail's son, Gordon, is a grown man with a family of his own. He told me about his parents.

"Mom and Dad told me, at an early age, about the adoption. Mother's eyes would shine and she would radiate her love for me. She had made me feel that I was the most important child on earth and the most special thing in their whole lives. Although I understood that someone had given me up so that I could be adopted, I never really felt the need to know who that someone was. I had a wonderful child-hood and now that I have children of my own, Mom and Dad are giving their special love to them as well. I know that some people who have been adopted have difficulty with the concept, that they were given up and unwanted. I thank God every day that I was wanted by these two wonderful people who are the finest parents that anyone could have."

As years ago we carried to your knees
The tales and treasures of eventful days,
Knowing no deed to humble to your praise,
Nor any gift too trivial to please,
So, still we bring—with older smiles and tears
What gifts we may, to claim the old, dear right;
Your faith, beyond the silence and the night,
Your love still close and watching through the
    years.

Kathleen Norris

*"You rear a child like you throw a ball," said
the country parson. "Give it the best shot you
can while it's in your hands, for it must go the
rest of the way by itself."*

My grandson, Marshall, and I had a good laugh over this little anecdote. Marshall insists that this story is a typical mother story.

The owner of a bakery was closing shop on a stormy winter's night when a man came in and asked for two sweet rolls. The baker was amazed that anyone would come out in such weather for just two sweet rolls.

"Are you married?" he asked.

"Of course," replied the man. "Do you think my mother would send me out on a night like this?"

My daughter, Julia, has friends who chose to adopt a youngster from Vietnam and when he arrived, he was a tiny, malnourished baby whose beautiful brown eyes held a lot of sadness.

With love and affection—and a good diet—Sean began to thrive and grow. When Sean was just eight months old, Patty found out that she was pregnant. Her blond-haired, blue-eyed son Mark was born and the two children, close in age, became close emotionally and formed a wonderful bond as only brothers can. When the boys were about four and five years old, they were in the park one day when an older child who had been listening to them talk looked at them strangely and said, "You guys are brothers?"

"Yeah," replied Mark. "One of us is adopted, but I always forget which one."

Patty could not have been happier.

How cherished the home where the family is valued and everyone knows he belongs.

Children are what the mothers are. No father's fondest care can fashion so the infant's heart.

W. S. Landor

Being a mother is an awesome responsibility. How do I raise my child to become a responsible, happy adult? When my first child was born, my mother gave me a beautiful, hand-written note that I cherish to this day.

My darling Edna,

How wonderful! You and George have a beautiful baby daughter. I am so proud of you!

I have been trying to think of any special advice that I could give to you that may help you in raising this marvellous gift from God. I was having much difficulty until I remembered something that your grandmother gave to me when you were born. She said to me, 'Your daughter will become what she sees in you. Jonathon Edwards, a clergyman, offers these five resolutions to live by. If you can live by these rules, your daughter will see in you a beautiful person, someone that she would like to be also.'

She gave me a card with these five resolutions:

1. I will live with all my might while I do live

2. I will never lose one moment of time, but will improve it in the most profitable way I possibly can

3. *I will never do anything which I should despise or think meanly of in another*

4. *I will never do anything out of revenge*

5. *I will never do anything which I should be afraid to do if it were the last hour of my life*

I have tried to live by this advice and when I look at you, my darling, I believe that I have been successful, for you are a kind, charming, wonderful young woman—the finest daughter any mother could ever hope to have.

I hope that Jonathon Edwards' wise words may bring something of your grandmother and I to you and your beautiful daughter Mary.

I love you very much!

Mother

Always remember to kiss your children goodnight, even if they are already asleep.

Early in this century, a young father loved to tell of his daughter's excited reaction when he told her she had a new baby sister.

"Does Mama know?" she asked her father on seeing the baby. "Let's go and tell her."

Here are some simple, yet wise words for all mothers.

A simple mother I must be,
To the little one who follows me,
I dare not ever go astray,
For fear she'll go the self-same way.
Remember—what she sees me do,
She might herself, try one day too.
She must believe I'm good and fine,
For she'll accept each word of mine,
A fault in me she must not see—
For I build for the years to be.

Children need models more than they need critics.

Joseph Joubert

Train up a child in the way he should go: and when he is grown, he will not depart from it.

Proverbs 22:6

My son-in-law, Bruce, reminded me this morning, "We learn from experience. A man never wakes up his second baby just to see him smile."

CELEBRATION OF MOTHERS

We, as Canadians, often hesitate to glorify the heroes and heroines of our country. As a result, the accomplishments of many who have had great influence on our heritage go unacknowledged.

One of these heroes is Dr. Marion Hilliard. Born on June 17, 1902, in Morrisburg, Ontario, she was one of five children. Atypically, her parents insisted that their daughters have the same education as their sons. Marion was an eager and apt pupil. She was determined to become a doctor and, in spite of much opposition, she graduated in 1927 with a Bachelor of Medicine from the University of Toronto.

She did post-graduate work in obstetrics and, after several years of study abroad, she returned to Toronto and joined the staff of Women's College Hospital. An outstanding obstetrician, she was appointed head of gynecology at that hospital in 1947.

Her work in this field produced many hundreds of healthy babies—each of whom she considered a part of her "family." She was always thrilled when some of her "babies" came back to visit as they grew into adulthood.

She passed away July 15, 1958. Her headstone reads simply: "Beloved Physician."

A baby is nothing but a bundle of possibilities.

Henry Ward Beecher

Raising children is like making biscuits: it is as easy to raise a big batch as one, while you have your hands in the dough.

E. W. Howe

The angels . . . singing unto one another can find among their burning terms of love, none so devotional as that of Mother.

Edgar Allan Poe

When you are a mother, you are never really alone in your thoughts. You are connected to your child and all those who touch your lives.

Sophia Loren

As a young wife and mother, so many years ago, the demands on my time were many. The wife of a minister was expected to attend a multitude of social functions that were a part of parish life. As well, I was expected to keep our children and our home spotless in case some member of the church community should stop by unexpectedly. It wouldn't do to have them think the minister's wife or family to be untidy.

For the most part, I kept up reasonably well. However, one particular Saturday, the girls and I were having a "day off." We stayed in bed together all morning—reading, knitting, and just having a restful time.

A knock on the door interrupted us and it was Julia, still in her nightdress, who scooted downstairs to open the door to Olive McCarthy—a pillar of the community—who had stopped by to return a book she'd borrowed earlier in the week.

I came down to greet her, my face red with mortification as I stammered out my excuses, "Children tired…no time to read…catching up on sleep…" and on and on.

Olive merely smiled and nodded, and left without staying for the cup of tea I had felt obliged to offer. I waited to hear what I was sure would be the inevitable remarks at church the next morning.

Instead, as Olive passed our family's pew, she nodded and handed me an envelope, saying, "I enjoyed seeing you and your family yesterday."

I opened the envelope and read her words:

Dear Edna,

Good for you! The time we have to spend with our children passes in the blink of an eye. How wise of you to make the most of it.

I thought you might enjoy this little poem.

Lord, give me patience when wee hands
Tug at me with their small demands.
Give me gentle and smiling eyes;
Keep my lips from hasty replies.
Let not weariness, confusion or noise
Obscure my vision of life's fleeting joys
So when, in years to come, my house is still
No bitter memories its rooms may fill.

*Mother love is the fuel that enables a normal
human being to do the impossible.*

M. C. Garretty

*We find delight in the beauty in the happiness
of children that makes the heart too big for the
body.*

Ralph Waldo Emerson

As mothers, we are often tempted to lecture our
children. Let us not forget Samuel Taylor
Coleridge's reminder:

*Advice is like the snow; the softer it falls, the
longer it dwells upon and the deeper it sinks
into the mind.*

Sometimes some small thing that we do can have an enormous impact on the future of our children.

The Depression winter of 1932 was a tough one for all of Canada, and no less so for the people of Saskatoon, Saskatchewan. It was there that Albert and Katherine Howe lived with their children, and during this difficult time the young couple were hard-pressed to feed their family. But when a young mother came to their door with a sack full of odds and ends to sell, Katherine gave her $1.50 so that the young woman could buy milk for her baby.

When Katherine emptied the bag a pair of small children's skates fell out. "Mine," said her four-year-old son. "No, mine!" cried his three-year-old sister Edna. They put on one skate each and went out to slide on the ice behind their home. After a week, Edna sold her share of the skates to her brother for a dime—and her brother Gordie Howe started his climb to the National Hockey League, where he became one of the finest players ever to play professional hockey.

What God is to the world, a mother is to her children.

Give a little love to a child and you get a great deal back.

THE HERITAGE BOOK

My dear friend, Eleanor, gave me this poem. She tells me that reading it brings back such fond memories of her own dear mother.

The morning sits outside afraid
Until my mother draws the shade;

Then it bursts in like a ball
Splashing sun all up the wall.

And the evening is not night
Until she's tucked me in just right
And kissed me and turned off the light.

Oh, if my mother went away
Who would start the night and day?

The laughter of a child is the light of the house

African proverb

Kind words can be short and easy to speak, but their echoes are truly endless.

Mother Teresa

It is not enough to love those who are near and dear to us. We must show them that we do so.

Lord Avebury

When you have children, life becomes a series of firsts: first words, first steps, first teeth, first haircuts—the list goes on.

How well I remember the story my friend Marion told me of her granddaughter's first haircut.

It was mid-December, the year that Marion's three grandchildren—John, 5, Kelly, 4, and Christy, 2—were to assist at the wedding of Marion's son-in-law's sister on the 22nd of December.

John, the ring bearer, would be wearing a tiny tuxedo, and the girls had beautiful red and white quilted dresses—perfect for a wedding so close to Christmas.

Because they were so young, their mother felt it was important to explain to them many times how the rehearsal and wedding would take place.

"First we'll go to Tony's to get our hair done, then we'll put on some nice clothes and go to the church to practise what you'll do at the wedding.

"The next afternoon, we'll go back to see Tony so he can make us beautiful again, and then you'll put on your wedding clothes and we'll go to the church.

"This all takes time—so you can't be pokey getting your clothes on."

Satisfied that they understood what would happen, their mother was relaxed, happy, and looking forward to the impending nuptials.

The Saturday before the wedding, the three children were playing in the playroom in their basement, while the youngest, Jamie, was being fed in the kitchen. Marion's daughter explained what happened then.

"I heard then coming up the stairs and Kelly was saying 'Boy, Mom is sure going to be happy that we won't need to go to Tony's before the wedding. It will save her lots of time.'

"The children came into the kitchen and I screamed! Kelly's long strawberry blond hair was hacked off to her chin level and Christy, who did not have a lot of hair to begin with, looked as if someone had chewed her hair off—her bangs were cut to her scalp in several places.

"I started to cry, and I could see that the children were utterly bewildered by my reaction to what they thought was something very helpful.

'Oh my gosh, the wedding is next week,' I must have said fifty times. I called our hairdresser, Tony, but was sobbing so hard it took several minutes for him to understand who was speaking and what had happened. He calmed me down when he said 'Bring them to me, I'm sure I can fix it.'

"I piled all four children into the car and headed off to town, where I hoped Tony would be able to salvage something of their hair.

"Tony did not disappoint me. At first he laughed, but when he saw how distraught I was, he was quick to reassure me."

"They'll look just fine—don't worry!"

"He was right," Marion told me. "The girls looked absolutely adorable—even Christy, whose already short hair was now even shorter. She had her first and second haircut in one day, but thanks to Tony's expertise, she looked beautiful and no one knew how awful her first haircut had been."

I do not love him because he is good, but because he is my little child.

Rabindranath Tagore

Religious words have value to the child only as experience in the home gives them meaning.

John Drescher

When you have children, you begin to understand what you owe your parents.

Japanese folk saying

THE HERITAGE BOOK

*How often thoughts and hearts return to a
home that's filled with love.*

*Love is the simple comfort and quiet happiness
of home.*

*To become a mother is not hard; to be a
mother is, however.*

*Mighty is the force of motherhood! It
transforms all things by its vital heat; it turns
timidity into fierce courage, and dreadless
defiance into tremulous submission; it turns
thoughtfulness into foresight, and yet stills all
anxiety into calm content; it makes selfishness
become self-denial and gives even to hard
vanity the glance of admiring love.*

George Eliot

*Family faces are magic mirrors. Looking at
people who belong to us we see the past,
present, and future.*

Gail Lumet Buckley

I find that statement to be so true. Many times as I look at my daughters, grandchildren or great-grandchildren, I will suddenly see something that reminds me of my own mother. It may be a gesture, a look, or something said, but seeing it will trigger a memory from so long ago.

Just recently, I was having a chat with my great-grandson, Justin. As he turned his face to me, the light caught his smile in such a way that he looked just like my late husband when he was Justin's age. For a moment it took my breath away, and then he turned again and the resemblance was gone.

It amazes me to think that some small part of me will be a part of my family generations in the future. I treasure that thought.

So many years ago, when cameras were new and few it was not uncommon for a family to have a photo taken but once a year, and that photo would be a formal family portrait.

Gradually, cameras became less complex and easier to use and families began to snap pictures not only at Christmas but all through the year.

Baby's first steps, fishing at the lake, or a visit to a museum in some far-off country were all subjects to be photographed again and again.

Many people—more organized than I—manage to keep their photos labelled and arranged beauti-fully in albums, also labelled for easy identification.

I have to admit that many of my photos are residing in large numbers of unmarked boxes awaiting the day that I organize them properly in albums.

My friend Mary McConnell has an excellent solution for this particular problem.

Mary and her husband are raising ten children, something almost unheard of in this day and age. Travelling with a family this size could be difficult at best. However, Mary has come up with an excellent idea to keep the children entertained on a long trip.

"Before we set off, we collect all of our loose photos and I buy several photo albums. We pass the hours in the van happily remembering the times pictured in the photos. We arrange the photos in the albums and, by the time we have finished, we have usually reached our destination—ready to make more memories."

If I am to arrange the photos that I now possess, I think I should need a trip around the world.

In times of quietness our hearts should be like trees, lifting their branches to the sky to draw down strength with which they will need to face the storms that will surely come.

Toyohiko Kagawa

Don't be annoyed when your children ask the impossible questions; be proud that they think you know the answers.

Believe the best rather than the worst. Children have a way of living up—or down— to your opinion of them.

We know how important it is to speak kindly to children. Children are able to sense very quickly our pleasure (or displeasure) with them. Soft, kind words go a long way in building a youngster's self-esteem. I enjoyed these wise words:

A little word of kindness spoken,
A motion or a tear,
Has often healed the heart that's broken
And made a friend sincere.
A word—a look—has crushed to earth
Full many a budding flower,
When had a smile but shown its worth,
It would brighten the dark hour.
Then deem it not an idle thing,
A pleasant word to speak,
The face you wear, the thought you bring,
A heart may heal or break.

Once some years ago, while I was at the supermarket, a young boy and his mother were walking ahead of me. As is often the case when young lads are shopping, he appeared to be daydreaming. His elbow banged into a display of pickles and several jars came crashing down to the floor. Pickles, juice, and glass were scattered across the aisle.

I braced myself for what I feared would be his mother's scolding. Instead, she handled the situation with tact and self-control.

She left her cart and ran to hug her son. "Have you hurt yourself?" she asked, and when he had assured her that he was fine, she went on. "That was too bad. Sometimes these things happen when we don't expect them to. Let's go and find someone who works here to help us clean up this mess."

She was calm and kind, and as I heard her speaking to the store manager, I knew that her understanding had helped her son through an embarrassing incident. He apologized for his carelessness and offered to pay for the damage. The manager declined his offer with thanks and the matter was closed with good feeling by all.

It seems to me that kindness works well in any situation.

Words have incredible power to build us emotionally. Most of us can clearly remember words of praise our parents spoke years ago.

CELEBRATION OF MOTHERS

If a man does not keep pace with his companions, perhaps it is because he hears a different drummer. Let him step to the music which he hears, however measured or far away.

Henry David Thoreau

How clever we would be, as parents, to heed this advice. How often a parent who is athletic tries to force a child into sports when the child's own interest lies in quiet reading.

Every child has potential in some direction. Wise is the parent who sees this potential and encourages it.

I like to tell the story of Lillian, a dear friend of mine, and her son, Alan. Lillian was an accomplished musician, a wonderfully talented lady who could play piano, violin, and flute (and most probably any another instrument she chose). After the untimely death of her husband, when Alan was but two years old, Lillian taught music to make ends meet.

She was determined that her young son should also be a musician, and she began his tutelage when he was very young. He proved to be an apt pupil and was able to play the piano and violin at a very early age. At first he loved to practise and would work for hours, needing little encouragement.

However, as he grew older, went to school, made good friends, and began to enjoy other activities, he seemed to spend a diminishing amount of time practising music. He played hockey with a neighbourhood team and became rather good at playing goal. His music practice time became less and less— and although Lillian was disappointed, she said very little.

Lillian, who knew next to nothing about the game of hockey, spoke with Alan's coach asking how she might be of some help to her son as he learned to play this game that he loved.

The coach told her that what a goaltender really needed was lots of practice stopping pucks. Lillian had never held a hockey stick, much less shot a puck, so she realized that this was not going to be of much help.

However, as a youngster, she had played baseball with her brother and had become quite proficient. For several evenings, she went to the basement and practised throwing a hockey puck the way she had thrown a baseball.

One day soon after, when Alan arrived home from school, Lillian asked if he would like to practise some hockey with her.

She took him to the basement where, to Alan's astonishment, she had drawn a net on the wall.

For the next hour, she threw puck after puck at her son, some high, some low, some hard and some bloopers that were difficult to catch. At the end of the hour both were exhausted but happy.

The two of them kept at this after-school regimen for the rest of the winter and Alan's skills improved tremendously. Over the next few years, Alan continued to play a lot of hockey and a little music.

Years passed and it was time for Alan to go off to university. Imagine his mother's surprise when he chose to major in music and not physical education. He explained it this way:

"My mother could have pushed me into music but instead she chose to encourage me in what I loved to do. Gradually I came to love music on my own and realized that music was what I wanted to do. I am thankful that my mother was wise enough to let me make my own choices. Not many parents would have done that."

Let him step to the music which he hears…

There are only two lasting bequests that we can hope to give our children. One of these is roots, the other is wings.

Hodding Carter

It's not what you think that influences your child; it is what you communicate.

*The most creative job in the world involves
taste, fashion, decorating, recreation,
education, transportation, psychology,
romance, cuisine, designing, literature,
medicine, handicraft, art, horticulture,
economics, government, community relations,
pediatrics, geriatrics, entertainment,
maintenance, purchasing, direct mail, law,
accounting, religion, energy, and management.
Anyone who can handle all of the above has to
be somebody special. She is. She's a mother.*

*It doesn't matter how old I get, whenever I see
something new or splendid, I want to call,
"Mom, come and look."*

Helen Exley

*Mother…she is their earth…she is their food
and their bed and their extra blanket when it
grows cold in the night; she is their warmth
and their shelter.*

Katherine Butler Hathaway

*Train up a child in the way he should go; and
when he is old, he will not depart from it.*

Proverbs 22:6

*A wise parent lets a child know what is
expected of him.*

In the tiny village of St. Aniset, Quebec, Mr. and
Mrs. Ernest Léger, shopkeepers, showed great
faith in their two sons. Instead of doling out their
allowance, the parents left the store's cash box open,
allowing the boys to help themselves to their
designated sums.

Some villagers felt this was an unfair temptation
and told the parents so. The Légeres saw it in a different light: as a daily testament to their faith and
trust.

It would seem that their faith was justified. The
older son, Paul Emile, became a Cardinal in the
Catholic church. The younger son, Jules, became a
Governor General of Canada.

*The most successful parents are those who
have the skill to get behind the eyes of the
child, seeing what he sees, thinking what he
thinks, feeling what he feels.*

Dr. James Dobson

*Saying yes to a child is like blowing up a
balloon. You have to know when to stop.*

*If you want to see both complete innocence
and the mystery of the ages, look into the eyes
of a baby.*

Bern Williams

"Each day is a gift, and a cause for celebrating
who we are, what we have achieved, and all
the joy we have yet to know." My mother shared
those words with me when I was very young. They
are words to live by.

*A child enters your home and for the next
twenty years makes so much noise that you
can hardly stand it. Then the child departs,
leaving the house so silent that you think you
are going mad.*

John Andrew Holmes

I have always been an admirer of the poetry of Edna
St. Vincent Millay. In all that I have read about
this talented woman, she credits much of her success
to the love and encouragement she received from
her beloved mother. She once told her mother: "I
am all the time talking about you and bragging, to
one person or another. I am like the Ancient
Mariner, who had a tale in his heart he must unfold
to all. I am always button-holing somebody and
saying 'Someday you must meet my mother!'"

CELEBRATION OF MOTHERS

*The God to whom little boys say their prayers
has a face very much like their mothers.*

Sir James Matthew Barrie

*Youth fades; love droops; the leaves of
friendship fall: a mother's secret love outlives
them all.*

Oliver Wendell Holmes

*All that I am or hope to be, I owe to my angel
mother.*

Abraham Lincoln

Many of the most wonderful moments that we spend with our children seem to come unexpectedly. Catching butterflies on a summer's afternoon, lying on the nighttime grass picking out the stars that make up the Big Dipper, building a snowman and using dad's best hat to top its head— all are happy memories that I have of times the girls and I enjoyed together.

One of my favourite recollections is of a summer's evening when the girls were very young. I had been baking all afternoon, making fresh bread and cookies for a parish tea on Saturday. The girls had been very good, playing on the swing in the yard and dressing the kitten in doll's clothes, but they had been coming into the house at frequent intervals.

"Mommy, Mommy come see.... Mommy guess what.... Mommy I want you to come outside.... Mommy, Mommy, Mommy!"

I turned a deaf ear to each of these pleas and continued with my baking.

The afternoon slipped away and soon the girls were in their nightgowns and ready for bed. I felt twinges of guilt as I tucked them into bed, but I was tired and justified myself—after all, it was just one afternoon.

I went out and sat on the porch and watched the sun setting in the distance. As I sat there, I saw a few little dots of light, and then more and more appeared until I felt that I was part of some heavenly galaxy. "The girls have to see this!" I thought. I went upstairs and woke them. They followed me down the stairs to the front door, where I told them to hold hands and shut their eyes. We went out the door and onto the porch.

"Now, open your eyes!"

Their little mouths fell open and sheer delight shone in their faces.

"Oh Mommy, it's beautiful!"

The four of us sat down on the wicker couch and watched with rapture the incredible sight.

I don't remember now how long we stayed on the porch that night, but I do know that the girls talked of little else for days after. Even now, we might be doing the dishes at a family gathering when one of the girls will say, "Do you remember the night Mom woke us up to see the fireflies?"

Sometimes we need to remind ourselves of what is really important in our lives. Sometimes we need to see the fireflies.

As much as I converse with sages and heroes, they have very little of my admiration. I long for rural and domestic sense, for the warbling of birds and for the prattling of little children.

John Adams

So often, when our children are young, it seems as if the work is endless. This next poem is to remind you how quickly childhood passes. My great-granddaughter, Bethany, presented this poem to her mother along with a plaster cast of her little hand.

When Beth's mother is old and grey, she will be able to pull them both out and remember the joys of her daughter's childhood.

Sometimes you get discouraged
Because I am so small
And always leave my finger prints
On furniture and walls.

But every day I'm growing up
And soon I'll be so tall
That all those little finger prints
Will be hard to recall.

So here's a plaster handprint,
So someday you can say,
"This is how your fingers looked
For Mother's Day in May."

Sometimes the things our children remember best from childhood are the simple rituals.

My daughter, Julia, and I were talking the other day when she said, "Do you know something that I loved when I was young? It was Saturday nights, listening to the hockey games."

Before the days of television, we would gather 'round the radio to listen to Foster Hewitt's wonderful play-by-play descriptions of what was happening on the ice—including his immortal "He shoots! He scores!"

Early in the day, George would make a huge pot of spaghetti and meatballs and delicious aromas would permeate every nook and cranny in the house. Promptly at six, we would sit down to this great meal. After dinner, while George and I did the dishes, the older girls would pop the popcorn and heat the milk for hot chocolate. Julia would pull George's armchair into the kitchen and place it near the radio. Julia loved to make herself comfortable on her dad's lap while the other girls and I would sit on the chairs around the kitchen table. Julia would then turn on the radio, and promptly at 8:00 we would hear the glorious words, "Good evening, hockey fans from across Canada."

We cheered ourselves hoarse for our beloved Toronto Maple Leafs and, for Julia, it remains another happy memory. In the words of Pierre Berton, "To me, ritual is the glue that keeps society together. Family rituals, like vacations with the whole family, are important things. To get a sense of community; that is what gives people peace of mind and security."

It's love that makes a house a home
And family life complete.
It's love that makes the good things good
And remembering them is sweet.

Rita Heyden

A home is built on dreams of the future, memories of the past and the ever present strength of a mother's love.

Gale Baker Stanton

Nothing's so dearly treasured
As the joy that families share,
Nothing's so reassuring
As just knowing others care…
Nothing's like a family
And the love that's always there.

Time seems to fly by when your children are young, and before you know it, they are heading off to school. If we have done our job well, our little ones will be eager to get there and enthusiastic about all there is to know about this experience. These next words describe so well my feelings as I watched each of my girls, in turn, begin the adventure known as schooling.

She's starting off to school today,
And because I love her so,
Like all the mothers in the world,
I hate to see her go.
Although I'm sure you understand
Such little ones as these,
Because she's all my hopes and dreams,
Do teach her gently please.

I do love these words from an unknown teacher: "A hundred years from now it will not matter what my bank account was, the sort of house I lived in or what kind of car I drove. But the world may be different because I was important in the life of a child."

As a parent, this would be a teacher that I would wish for my children to have.

My husband, George, would always offer a prayer for teachers on the first Sunday in September, when the children would be returning to class:

Grant we beseech thee, O heavenly Father, to all who teach in our schools, the spirit of wisdom and grace, that they may lead their pupils to reverence, truth, desire goodness and rejoice in beauty; so that all may come to know and worship thee, the giver of all that is good; through Jesus Christ our Lord.

Next to a parent, a teacher is probably the person with the most influence on a child's life. A teacher possesses a rare gift—the ability to shape young minds in wisdom through gentle patience.

One of the finest teachers that I know is Bev Hall, a lovely young woman teaching in our local school. Bev has no children of her own, but she explained it this way: "All of the children that I teach I consider to be mine. I put so much of myself into teaching them each day that I'm afraid I would have nothing left to give any children of my own." This poem is a tribute to Bev and all the fine teachers across the country.

God gave you that rarest gift
An understanding heart,
A gentle kindly manner,
Your wisdom to impart

Oh some men build well with steel and iron,
To pave their way to fame,
But you are building character,
A lasting tribute to your name.

The lives you touch, the good you do,
Shall never know an end,
And we are proud to call you
Our teacher and our friend.

M. Griswold

Thinking about school and education reminds me of Daisy Sands Rittgers, a wife, mother, grand-mother, great-grandmother—and now a university graduate.

Daisy was a freshman at Eastern Illinois University in 1927. She was doing extremely well in her courses when illness and then the stock market crash forced her to withdraw from school.

Teachers in those days did not need to have a university degree, and so Daisy looked for, and found, a job teaching in a school in Illinois.

Daisy was a born teacher! She loved her job and the children adored her. Time passed, and Daisy married and raised a family while continuing her teaching career.

Finally, at age 75, she retired. All through her career, though, and even into retirement, she felt that something had been left unfinished. And so it was that in the summer of 1996, Daisy enrolled once more at Eastern Illinois University, working hard to complete the courses that would grant her a university degree.

It was with great pride on Sunday, August 4, 1996, that Daisy Sands Rittgers proudly walked across the stage to a standing ovation from her classmates, family, friends, and the staff, where the Board of Governors' Degree was conferred—some sixty-nine years after she had started.

My grandson, Marshall, contributed this poem, given to him by his mother Marg.

A CRADLE SONG

The angels are stooping
Above your bed;
They weary of trooping
With the whimpering dead.
God's laughing in Heaven
To see you so good;
The Sailing Seven
Are gay with His mood.
I sigh then I kiss you,
For I must own
That I shall miss you
When you have grown.

William Butler Yeats

A mother is not a person to lean on but a person to make leaning unnecessary.

Dorothy Canfield Fisher

CELEBRATION OF MOTHERS

A mother's children are like ideas; none are as wonderful as her own.

Chinese fortune

They always looked back before turning the corner, for their mother was always at the window to nod and smile and wave her hand at them. Somehow, it seemed as if they couldn't get through the day without that, for whatever their mood might be, their last glimpse of that motherly face was sure to affect them like sunshine.

Louisa May Alcott

Whatever is worth doing at all is worth doing well.

Earl Phillip of Chesterfield

This is a concept that is sometimes difficult to convey to young students.

As a youngster, my brother, Ben, was always in a hurry to get things done. He often turned in school projects that were less than his best efforts. My father had a story he told in the hope of inspiring Ben to better efforts. I remember it well and have found myself using it with my children and grandchildren when I feel that circumstances warrant.

When the Athenian sculptor, Phidias, was carving the statue of Athena to be placed in the Acropolis, he spent considerable time working on the back of the statue's head. He was careful to carve each strand of hair so that it stood out as far as possible.

Someone watching remarked, "That figure will stand a hundred feet high with its back to the marble wall. Who will ever know what details you are putting behind there?"

The sculptor replied, "I will know." And he continued with his detailed chiselling.

It's a funny thing about life; if you refuse to accept anything but the best, you very often get it.

W. Somerset Maugham

A mother's advice:

Frame anything your child brings home from his first day of school.

Get to know your child's teachers.

Make sure that your children arrive at school on time each day.

Read to your children every day.

CELEBRATION OF MOTHERS

Children need to be accountable. Let them accept the consequences for their actions.

Teach your children respect for their teachers and the other people who work hard to make their school an enjoyable place to be.

Encourage your child to participate in extra-curricular activities and attend every one that you can.

Do your best to be consistent and fair when dealing with your children.

Never miss an opportunity to tell your children how much you love them.

I touch the future. I teach.

Christa McAuliffe

My heart is singing for joy this morning. A miracle has happened! The light of understanding has shone upon my little pupil's mind and behold, all things are changed.

Anne Sullivan,
on her breakthrough with Helen Keller

No bubble is so iridescent or floats longer than that blown by a successful teacher.

Sir William Osler

One looks back with appreciation to the brilliant teachers, but with gratitude to those who touched our human feelings. The curriculum is so much necessary raw material, but warmth is the vital element for the growing plant and for the soul of the child.

Carl Jung

The aim of education is to teach you how to think, not what to think.

From an early age, children today are offered an enormous selection of activities to become involved in. The most numerous, of course, are athletics, and it seems as if the ages at which youngsters are getting involved in organized sports are becoming younger and younger. Most often this is not a problem, but there are occasions when children are pushed to be competitive too early. It is sometimes necessary to take a step back and decide who really wants to excel, parent or child.

Neighbours of ours have a young daughter who is a very talented figure skater. They have been approached by several coaches who seem to think that Michelle is world champion material. Happily, Michelle's parents are realistic and are speaking with a number of experts, including parents of other elite athletes, before they become very excited (or worried) about her athletic future.

Pat explained to me what she and her husband feel are the most important things they have learned about having an elite athlete in the family.

"The crucial thing," said Pat, "is to keep predictions of glory in perspective. Real talent in most sports isn't easily identified before puberty. Growth and development will affect the child's ability in most sports.

"You must also be sure that your child loves her sport and wants to do it. There is a fine line between a supportive parent and one who is pushy. She needs to be motivated by her needs, not ours.

"Choosing a good coach is also a most important task. The coach should be interested in our child as a person—not just as an athlete. The coach needs to develop potential while being sure that the sport remains enjoyable.

"Once the coach has been chosen, the job of training needs to be left to the coach, without parental interference.

"The single most important point we've heard is that our child needs to know that we love her for who she is, not for what she does or how she performs."

I think that Michelle is very fortunate to have a mother and father who are proud of their daughter's accomplishments but who love her for herself.

Sports do not build character. They reveal it.

Heywood Brown

When you encourage a young athlete you must set aside your dreams for them to help them attain their own dream.

Each athlete involved in the Special Olympics repeats this oath: "Let me win. But if I cannot win let me be brave in the attempt." It seems to me that this could be an oath for us all to live by.

It is interesting to note that girls are now much more involved in sports that used to be considered "male only."

Friends of ours have a son and three daughters, all of whom have played hockey. John began in the house league and Kelly played for the local girls' team. Their two younger sisters Christy and Jamie were also eager to play but were too young for the girls' team, and when their mother approached the executives of the boys' house league she was told that girls were not welcome.

Undeterred, their mother went to a nearby town where she was able to convince a more open-minded group to allow her daughters to play.

Mom and dad took the girls to the arena for their first game.

As the girls entered the dressing room before the game several of their male teammates made comments. "Why do we have yucky girls on the team?" "How come we have to have girls and the Blue team doesn't?" The little girls said nothing—but Jamie, who was very shy, was near tears.

However, much to the boys' surprise, the girls were excellent skaters and dominant factors in the game. The game ended with a 7–1 win, with Christy scoring four goals and Jamie three.

On the way off the ice the opposing team was taunted with cries of "Too bad you don't have girls on *your* team!"

Christy and Jamie played one season in the boys' house league before they were invited to play for the local girls' team.

The hockey story doesn't end there. All three of the girls continued to play hockey at a high level and each, in turn, was awarded a scholarship to a university in the United States, where they received an outstanding education while continuing to play the game that they loved so much.

All across our country mothers who used to spend hours in an arena cheering for their sons are now spending equal time encouraging their daughters in this wonderful Canadian game.

I can't help but admire the mothers who have, through their persistence, made this possible.

Don't limit a child to your own learning, for he was born in another time.

Rabbinical saying

For when the One Great Scorer comes to mark against your name, He writes—not that you won or lost—but how you played the game.

Grantland Rice

Use what talents you possess; the woods would be very silent if no birds sang there except those that sang best.

Henry Van Dyke

CELEBRATION OF MOTHERS

A mother can't change the colour of her child's eye, but she can help give the eyes the light of understanding and the warmth of sympathy. She can't much alter her child's features, but she can in many ways endow them with the glow of humaneness, kindness and friendliness... which may in the long run bring a lot more happiness than the perfection that wins beauty contests.

Anonymous

Despite the new techniques in raising children, nothing seems to work like an old fashioned mother's firm exclamation, "Move, if you know what's good for you."

By the time a mother quits worrying about how her children will turn out, it's time to worry about when they'll come in.

Feel the dignity of a child. Do not feel superior to him, for you are not.

Robert Henri

You have a wonderful child. Then, when he is thirteen, gremlins carry him away and leave,

*in his place, a stranger who gives you not a
moment's peace.*

Jill Eikenberry

For many parents, the "terrible twos" are replaced
by the "terrible teens."

One of the more difficult aspects of being a
minister's child is dealing with peers who assign the
role of "goodie goodie."

Our daughters Mary and Marg dealt fairly well
with this problem. Julia had more difficulty. She felt
compelled to prove that she could be as "bad" as her
friends. Fortunately, her friends were a nice group of
youngsters, so "bad" became a relative term. George
and I accepted her rebelliousness quite easily—in
fact, I think George was secretly quite pleased to see
his daughter accepted as one of the group.

There was only one time that we really had to lay
down the law. Julia's friends had begun to smoke,
and suddenly Julia was lighting up too.

George took Julia aside and spoke to her quietly
but firmly.

"If you truly enjoy smoking, Julia, then that is
your choice. You may not smoke in our home, but I
won't forbid you to smoke elsewhere," he said. "But,
if you are smoking to be one of the gang, I hope you
will decide against it."

From that day to this, Julia never smoked again.

CELEBRATION OF MOTHERS

When all else fails, console yourself by saying "It's just a phase."

H. Jackson Brown, Jr.

Never break off communications with a teenager, no matter what they do.

A. Picard

When I was a boy of fourteen, my father was so ignorant that I could hardly stand to have him around me. Then, when I got to be twenty-one, I was astonished at how much he had learned in only seven years.

Mark Twain

Oh, to be only half as wonderful as my child thought I was when he was small, and only half as stupid as my teenager now thinks I am.

Rebecca Richards

Treat your children with the same respect that you want them to give you.

E. Leatherland

Before I got married, I had theories about bringing up children; now I have six children and no theories.

John Wilmont

The young always have the same problem—how to rebel and conform at the same time. They have now solved this by defying their parents and copying one another.

Quentin Crisp

Don't laugh at youth for his affectations; he's only trying on one face after another until he finds his own.

Logan Pearsall Smith

It's all that the young can do for the old, to shock them and keep them up to date.

George Bernard Shaw

My good friend Mary McConnell and I had a very interesting discussion about the difficulty of raising teenagers. Mary was particularly upset with one of her sons, who had come in late and neglected to phone home.

"You know, Edna, I was happy to see him but I had been so worried it was only my anger that showed. I shouted quite loudly about his inconsiderateness. He felt very badly and, after my tirade, so did I."

As we talked, I remembered a booklet designed to explain parents to teenagers. It begins with a translation of parents' comments. For example, if a parent says "This is a fine time to be getting home!" it means, "I've been worried about you. When you don't let me know you'll be late, I sit here imagining all sorts of awful things happening to you."

Mary bought the book for her son.

Children want some honest direction. They want a set of sensible rules to live by. The time has come to dust off the rule book.

Jenkins Lloyd Jones

My grandson Fred and his wife June have two sons, Mickey and Geoffrey. When the two were younger June cut an article from the newspaper and stuck it on the door of the refrigerator. Whenever the boys were particularly fractious she would direct them to read the list. It was a wonderfully wise and ironic list of rules titled "How to Raise a Juvenile Delinquent in Your Own Family." Here are a few of the highlights.

Begin with infancy to give the child everything he wants. This will ensure his believing that the world owes him a living.

When he uses obscene words, laugh heartily at him. Soon he'll acquire a vocabulary that will blow your ears off.

Pick up everything he leaves lying around. This will teach him that he can always pass off responsibility to others.

Take his part against neighbours, teachers, policemen. They are all prejudiced against your son. He is never wrong.

Prepare yourself for a life of grief. Following these rules you will surely have it.

I do beseech you to direct your efforts more to preparing youth for the path and less to preparing the path for the youth.

Ben Lindsay

We often tend to lump teenagers into the "difficult" category. Not so my friend Emily. When her husband passed away, leaving her alone in a large home in Philadelphia, it could have been overwhelming—except for a group of teenage neighbours.

"After John's death, I couldn't seem to cope with even the most simple tasks. It was too much trouble to take out the trash. I couldn't mow the lawn, much less keep up the gardens.

"Then about two weeks after the funeral, I awoke to the noise of a lawnmower—my lawnmower. I looked out the window and there was an army of young people mowing, pulling weeds, clipping the hedges, all laughing and talking together. I went down to the front door where Mark, our closest neighbour, explained."

"Good morning, Mrs. Stone," he said. "We had nothing much to do today, so we thought we'd give you a hand with some of the chores."

"Well, I couldn't help it. I started to cry. He put his arm around me and said, 'Mrs. Stone, we really miss Mr. Stone and we wanted to do something to show how much we cared. My mom suggested something practical and we all agreed.'

"These wonderful young people helped me keep up my home until I was ready to move into a condominium. Even after I had moved, many continued to come and visit me, bringing a sunshine that only the young can provide."

Teenagers difficult? Definitely not so, according to Emily.

Blessed is the influence of one true, loving human soul on another.

George Eliot

Nothing is so infectious as example.

Charles Kingsley

We shall make a new rule of life from tonight: always try to be a little kinder than is necessary.

Sir James Matthew Barrie

Trouble is, kids feel they have to shock their elders and each generation grows up into something harder to shock.

Cal Craig

This poem is one of my favourites from the work of Edna St. Vincent Millay. I believe that mothers of teenagers could take her words to their hearts.

The courage that my mother had
Went with her, and is with her still:
Rock from New England quarried;
Now granite in a granite hill.

CELEBRATION OF MOTHERS

The golden brooch my mother wore
She left behind for me to wear;
I have no thing I treasure more:
Yet, it is something I could spare.

Oh, if instead she'd left to me
The thing she took into the grave!—
That courage like a rock, which
She has no more need of, and I have.

All children wear the sign: "I want to be important NOW!" Many of our juvenile delinquency problems arise because nobody reads the sign.

Dan Pursuit

If a child lives with approval, he learns to live with himself.

Dorothy Law Nolte

I think you might enjoy this description of "modern" youth.

"Our youths love luxury. They have bad manners, contempt for authority; they show disrespect for their elders, and love to chatter in place of exercise.

Children are now tyrants, not servants of their households. They no longer rise when their elders enter the room. They contradict their parents, chatter before company, gobble up their food, and tyrannize their teachers."

"Written by a mother of today," you might think. In actual fact, it was written by Socrates, the Greek philosopher, around 400 B.C. The more things change, the more they stay the same.

If parents want honest children, they should be honest themselves.

Robert Ingersoll

The development of strong character must be emphasized and rewarded in the home.

Charles Stanley

My own contact with teenagers today is very positive. At Christmas time, many of the young people in our area do a great service for the shut-ins, or people who are hospitalized. These young men and women provide a volunteer service that does Christmas shopping and wrapping for anyone who is unable, for whatever reason, to do their own.

What a relief for these people to know that, in spite of their incapacity, their Christmas will still be a joyous time of giving because of the help received from the teens.

The teenagers enjoy this service as well. John, a young neighbour of ours, told me that he has never enjoyed Christmas shopping as much as when he was "volunteer shopping."

It is easy to have faith in the world of tomorrow, when I see the youth of today.

Parents are the bones on which children cut their teeth.

Peter Ustinov

If you want your children to keep their feet on the ground, put some responsibility on their shoulders.

Dear Abby

The teenagers in my family, my great-grandchildren, Justin and Jenny, also make me very proud.

When they were in middle school, they each submitted their name to be "twinned" with a resident in our local nursing home. Their first visit was a "get acquainted" ice cream party, where they were introduced to their "twins" in a social setting. They made ice cream sundaes and then spent time getting to know one another.

Early in December, the children and their older companions were transported by bus to the local mall, where the students helped with window browsing and Christmas shopping. When they returned to the home, they had a wonderful time wrapping parcels and singing Christmas carols.

They went on several other outings, including a Christmas concert at the school, and a tour of homes ablaze with Christmas lights. A highlight was the Christmas dinner prepared and served by the students in the week before Christmas.

During this time, Justin and Jenny became very attached to their elderly companions and were not ready to break off their friendship when the holiday period ended.

They kept up their visits, usually once or twice a week. I worried that when the two entered high school and more demands were placed on their time perhaps they would not be able to visit their friends as often. I worried needlessly. No matter how busy their weeks, they always managed to make time to visit the home and the elderly people who have become such an important part of their lives.

I find it very gratifying that my grandchildren show such a caring and giving nature.

CELEBRATION OF MOTHERS

*I expect to pass through this world but once.
Any good, therefore, that I can do, or any
kindness that I can show to my fellow creature,
let me do it now. Let me not defer or neglect it,
for I shall not pass this way again.*

Stephan Grellet

*Our children are likely to live up to what we
believe of them.*

Lady Bird Johnson

*A wonderful motto for teens and parents is to
never needlessly harm the respect of one
another.*

Dr. Kay Kuzma

Our children are the messages to the future.

Billy Graham

Every day of your life is a page of your history.

Arabic folk saying

Children provide us with a never-ending supply of special moments. It may be as simple as a flower given on a summer's day or as complex as a surprise anniversary party.

Sometimes, one such brief time may be especially poignant.

I was thinking today of a lovely young girl that I knew for too short a time.

Alysia Gabriel was born July 20, 1979. When she was diagnosed, at five months of age, with cystic fibrosis—that horrible disease that attacks children and young adults—her parents, who knew little about the disease, decided that they would fight it with her and help her win.

Alysia put her efforts into fundraising at a very early age.

When she was five years old, she appeared as the C.F. poster child and she took part regularly in radiothons and many community events to raise funds for research.

In all of the projects that Alysia (known as "Lou" to her friends) did along the way, she felt that she was achieving something and helping other C.F. sufferers. She hoped and wished for a cure—and she was making a difference.

I met Alysia when she was a vivacious high school cheerleader. My friend and I often watched the football games and Alysia would come bouncing over to say hello. Her enthusiasm and *joie de vivre* simply radiated from her, and her beautiful smile would melt any heart.

Alysia worked tirelessly for the C.F. foundation, and many of her fundraising activities were done with members of the Toronto Blue Jays baseball team.

At one particular fundraising dinner, Alysia spoke with candour of a day in the life of a C.F. sufferer. She told of the many pills to be taken, of the clapper (the machine used to pound on the back and loosen secretions in the lungs), and of being endlessly tired at the end of a day from working so hard to breathe. Her speech showed no self-pity, nor was it maudlin—many times she used humour and her ever-present smile to make a point. At the end of her speech, Joe Carter, first baseman for the Blue Jays, sat mesmerized, tears pouring down his cheeks, as he listened to this young girl's courageous story.

On July 20, 1995, Alysia was selected to throw out the ceremonial first pitch at the Blue Jays game in the Skydome in Toronto.

With her proud mother, Michelle, and brother Barrett looking on, thousands of fans stood and cheered as Alysia threw the ball to home plate.

It is a memory that all of us cherish.

Just one year later, on the morning of her seventeenth birthday, Alysia succumbed to the disease she had fought against so valiantly. She has died, but her memory will live in the hearts of all

whom she touched in her short life. I feel grateful to
have been one of those people.

*God gave us memories that we might have
roses in December.*

Sir James Matthew Barrie

*If we celebrate the years behind us, they
become stepping stones of the strength and joy
for the years ahead.*

*The guardian angels of life sometimes fly so
high as to be beyond our sight, but they are
always looking down upon us.*

Jean Paul Richter

*The best thing about the future is that it comes
only one day at a time.*

Abraham Lincoln

*The highest reward for a person's toil is not
what she gets for it, but rather, what she
becomes from it.*

CELEBRATION OF MOTHERS

The three grand essentials of happiness are: something to do, something to love, and something to hope for.

Thomas Chalmers

People are like stained glass windows: they sparkle and shine when the sun is out, but when the darkness sets in, their true beauty is revealed only if there is light within.

Elizabeth Kubler-Ross

Line by line, moment by moment, special times are etched into our memories in the permanent ink of everlasting relationships.

Gloria Gaither

Reach high, for stars lie hidden in your soul. Dream deep, for every dream precedes the goal.

Ralph Waldo Emerson

Happiness is found along the way, not at the end of the journey.

I know not what the future holds, but I know who holds the future.

My grandson, Marshall, is a lawyer, and a very good one at that. It took some doing, on his parents' part, however, to keep him interested in school and putting forth his best efforts in order to qualify for law school. As with many young people, his outside interests often seemed to be taking precedence over his school work. At the time, Marshall frequently resented his parents' "interference" in his life. Now, of course, he realizes just what a wonderful influence and help they were for him.

Many parents don't always hold on to their values when it seems easier to simply give in to the wishes of their children. What a disservice we do them when we give in always. It may be a more difficult decision to stand by these values, but when we stand firm both child and parent benefit.

Marshall often expressed his thanks to his parents but he also chose to give them a tangible expression of his appreciation.

For many years Marg and Bruce had shared a dream of visiting England. When Marshall presented his parents with two first-class tickets to London, England, they were completely overwhelmed.

"Mom, you made me do my homework every night. Because of you, my dream came true. The least I can do is give you your dream."

When our neighbour Debbie was young, her mother returned to work in order to help the family make ends meet. Her mother was gone early and often returned just around dinner hour, but Debbie never felt neglected. Her mother chose to leave notes for her to find all over the house.

On the refrigerator would be a note. "Hi Deb. I love you. Help yourself to some veggies and dip for a snack."

On the television might be a message. "Don't even think about turning on the television, you little rascal, until your homework is done! Love Mom."

Even as Debbie moved on to high school the notes continued: In a lunch bag—"Good luck on your test!" or in her closet—"Thanks for keeping your cupboard so neat."

When her mother passed away from cancer, Debbie was devastated. But even when she was gone her loving influence lived on. Debbie began finding notes of love and encouragement in odd places—in an encyclopedia, a cookbook, or under the bathroom sink.

When Debbie was to be married she chose to wear her mother's antique pearls. When she opened the box, there she found a note attached: "I am so happy for you darling! Wear these pearls for luck and know that I am with you on this special day."

We are here to help each other, to try to make each other happy.

Give the best you've got today. That's a better recipe for a better tomorrow.

The uncertainties of the present always give way to the enchanted possibilities of the future.

The best thing about the future is that it comes only one day at a time.

Time passes quickly. There is nothing we can do about this except to see that, as far as possible, it passes fruitfully. If in passing it lays up its store of good deeds done, noble ambitions clung to heroically and kindness and sympathy scattered with a lavish hand, there will always be given to it a permanence and enduring quality that nothing can take away. Take time to look—it is the price of success. Take time to think—it is a source of power. Take time to play—it is the secret of perennial youth. Take time to read—it is the source of wisdom. Take time to be friendly—it is the way to happiness. Take time to laugh—it is the music of the soul.

I took those words from a sermon given by my husband, George, to send to my daughter Julia.

Julia is an executive for a large multi-national corporation and she feels, on occasion, that she is so busy that time for herself is almost impossible to find.

We had spent some considerable time on the phone talking about this problem and I felt at a loss to know how to advise her.

Thankfully, whenever I'm unsure I can usually find something helpful in the wise words of my husband's sermons.

I hope that Julia will find them to be of help to her.

Kind words are the music of the world. They have a power which seem to be beyond natural causes, as though they were some angel's song which had lost its way and come to earth.

No man or woman of the humblest sort can really be strong, gentle, pure, and good without the world being better for it, without somebody being helped and comforted by the very existence of that goodness.

Philip Brooks

*There will come a time when you believe
everything is finished. That will be the
beginning.*

Louis L'Amour

*Success is important, but so is the way we
arrive there.*

Bern Williams

*The best way to succeed in life is to act on the
advice you give others.*

Some of the happiest times that I remember as a
child, mother, grandmother, and great-
grandmother are those days and weeks passed
together on a family vacation.

In a minister's home there was seldom much
money, with salaries being extremely low. However,
somehow my mother and father would manage to
save enough each year so that we could take a trip
together. We were especially fortunate because my
mother's family was quite well-to-do and Grandma
and Grandpa Milne would make sure that a birthday
or anniversary card contained "a little something for
your holiday."

My father felt that travel was the best form of
education, and whenever he and mother had
decided on our destination, Father would read up on

the history of the area, and for several months before our departure our dinner conversations would centre around various points of interest or interesting facts or other information. He would also be sure to tell us of anything of importance that we would pass en route.

Ben, Sarah, and I would be totally delighted if we were the first to spot something that father had mentioned to us prior to departure. Father would be equally thrilled to find a point of interest just as it had been described in his book of information.

The nicest part of our travels, of course, was that we children had the undivided attention of our parents, something that was quite rare during the rest of the year in a busy parish.

How wonderful it was to enjoy simple pleasures all together; an afternoon picnic on the beach, a walk through the forest, or sitting on the porch watching the stars come out.

It also gave our parents an enjoyable chance to be close, as well. While we children swam in a lake or built sand castles on a beach, mother and father would talk together endlessly, again a rare pleasure during the rest of the year.

These vacations were a time of family togetherness and brought us joyful memories that would last us a lifetime.

Many a time during the long cold winter we could lighten an evening with, "Do you remember when…" and then go on to remind ourselves of something wonderful from our vacation of the previous summer.

Ben, Sarah, and I still talk about those happy times together, and will probably do so until the end of our lives.

If you want to give your children something special you can probably not find a better gift than a family vacation.

For my part, I travel not to go anywhere, but to go. I travel for travel's sake. The great affair is to move.

Robert Louis Stevenson

My favourite thing is to go where I've never been.

Diane Arbus

When you travel, remember that a foreign country is not designed to make you comfortable. It is designed to make its own people comfortable.

Clifton Fadiman

CELEBRATION OF MOTHERS

Travel is fatal to prejudice, bigotry and narrow-mindedness.

Mark Twain

At the end of your life you will never regret not having passed one more test, not winning one more verdict, or closing one more deal. You will regret time not spent with a husband, a friend, a child, or a parent.

Barbara Bush

One of our family's most memorable vacations occurred the year before my husband George passed away.

He decided that it would be a wonderful idea to have a "family reunion" vacation—a get-together for all of our extended family, including aunts, uncles, cousins, etc.

Since none of us had a property large enough to accommodate such a numerous group, George made arrangements for all of us to meet at a provincial campsite, thankfully one that boasted indoor toilet and shower facilities.

The family began to assemble on the Friday evening accompanied by squeals of, "Oh my, you look wonderful!" or "Look how the children have grown."

By Saturday morning nearly one hundred of our relatives had pitched their tents and were setting up picnic tables for a hearty "pot-luck" breakfast.

The children, many of whom had never met each other, were making tentative overtures of friendship by playing baseball or skipping rope together.

After breakfast many families took time to visit from tent to tent or picnic table to picnic table greeting family members and catching up on months (or years) of news.

George (organizer of many a parish picnic) had arranged a number of different games involving both adults and children in large teams. There were three-legged races, sack races, pass the peach (no hands allowed!) and, the most popular, the raw egg toss.

Saturday evening the men got together and cooked a variety of chicken, steak, and fish on an enormous barbecue while the ladies made salads of all kinds.

It was a wonderful meal made even more delightful by the conversations held with seldom-seen family members from across the country.

One of the highlights of the reunion was the campfire on Saturday evening. George and the other men built an enormous fire and the children toasted marshmallows and sticks, family members took turns telling stories that were, in most cases, amusing— or interesting or occasionally sad, but always about the family. It was like being part of a living scrapbook of family history.

On Sunday we joined together for a service of worship followed by a brunch, featuring all of our leftovers.

As we packed up to go home it was with regret that our time together had been so short, but with the joy of having had so many of us reunited.

There is really nothing that can replace your family and its love that makes the memories of family times so sweet.

Recall it as often as you wish, a happy memory never wears out.

Libbie Fudim

Every family has its own history, its own heartbeat…a family is where life begins and love happens.

Write in your heart that every day is the best day in the year.

Ralph Waldo Emerson

Good family life is never an accident, but always an achievement by those who share it.

J. Brossard

A placid face and a gentle tone will make my family more happy than anything else I can do for them.

E. J. King

Tradition gives us a sense of solidarity and roots, knowing there are some things one can count on.

Gloria Gaither

May is often the time of year when parents start thinking of plans for their children's summer vacation. In many families these plans include summer camp. There are many wonderful camps with extraordinary facilities for swimming, sailing, water skiing and all of the other activities that youngsters enjoy on warm summer days.

Several years ago, I heard of a new and interesting camp for grandparents and their grandchildren. It is set in a traditional camp setting, in the woods by a lake. There are sleeping cabins and a large mess hall for meals. The difference is that the children stay together with a counsellor, in cabins, while the grandparents stay in rooms much like a small motel.

Children and their grandparents eat together and participate in many of the camp activities, such as sailing, or campfire wiener roasts. It can be a

precious time for all, without the grandparents having the responsibility of making meals or having to keep up the pace of the youngsters.

I think it is a wonderful, innovative idea that I hope to take advantage of one day.

"Fun is always just around the corner when you have a grandchild."

These lovely lines came to my mind today as I thought of my mother.

Where there is love the heart is light,
Where there is love the day is bright,
Where there is love there is a song
To help when things are going wrong
Where there is love there is a smile
To make all things seem more worthwhile.
Where there is love there's quiet peace,
A tranquil place where turmoils cease
Love changes darkness into light
And makes the heart take "wingless flight"
And Mothers have a special way
Of filling homes with love each day,
And when the home is filled with love
You'll always find God spoken of,
And when a family "prays together"

That family also "stays together,"
And once again a Mother's touch
Can mould and shape and do so much
To make this world a better place
For every colour, creed, and race
For when man walks with God again
There shall be peace on earth for men.

*A mother's love is indeed the golden link that
binds youth to age; and he is still but a child,
however time may have furrowed his brow,
who can yet recall, with a softened heart, the
fond devotion or the gentle chidings of the best
friend that God ever gave us.*

N. Bovee

My daughter Mary sent along the following piece
by Bette-Jane Raphael. Her daughter
Elizabeth gave it to her, but as she said, "I think it
applies to most mother–daughter relationships."

*One of the precious payoffs of being a
daughter is that as we get older, our mothers
seem to get better and better.*

*The lessons they sometimes had to drive home
to us with brickbats suddenly make perfect
sense. The advice that once seemed colossally*

*and hopelessly outdated becomes recognizable
as the wisdom we refused to see. And the
person who might once have been looked upon
as life's chief roadblock—the adversary we
were put on this earth to overcome—stands
revealed as none other than the friend and ally
that, in truth, she always was.*

John Wesley, the founder of the Methodist church, remembered his father once asking his mother, "How can you have the patience to tell that blockhead John the same thing twenty times over?"

"Why Samuel," his mother, Susana, replied, "if I had only told him nineteen times, I would have wasted my breath."

*And so our mothers and grandmothers have,
more often than not, anonymously handed on
the creative spark, the seed of the flower they
themselves never hoped to see—or like a sealed
letter they could not plainly read.*

Alice Walker

*"You almost died," a nurse told her. But that
was nonsense. Of course she wouldn't have
died; she had children. When you have
children, you're obligated to live.*

Anne Tyler

Happy the son whose faith in his mother remains unchanged.

Louisa May Alcott

There are few days in a young person's life that are more exciting than the day they leave for university.

I remember particularly the day that my grandson, Marshall, "set sail" for the University of Western Ontario. It was a red-letter day indeed!

Marshall was an extremely bright young man, but throughout his school career, it was a constant battle to keep him focused on his studies. There were many days when Marg and Bruce were at their wits' end and almost ready to give up on him. Thankfully, they persisted and Marshall's marks gradually began to rise—to a barely acceptable level.

When the football coach from the university came to visit and suggested that if Marshall could boost his marks, he would undoubtedly have a starting position on the team, there was no holding him back.

Over the course of his final year in high school he managed to make the honour role—the first time this had happened since he was in Grade 5.

When the letter of acceptance arrived from the university I'm not sure who was more excited, Marshall or his parents.

And then, it was time for him to leave.

As Marg hugged her son she was suddenly overwhelmed and her tears began to flow.

Marshall, thinking her tears were tears of sadness, began to console her. "Ah, Mom, don't cry. I know you'll miss me but I'll be coming home some weekends—please don't cry."

When she finally gained control, Marg explained, "Marshall, these are tears of joy! A few years ago this was a day I thought I would never see. When your dad and I nagged, cajoled, threatened, and coerced you to do your schoolwork, it wasn't an easy time for us. Many days I just wanted to give up and let you do your own thing. But something of your grandmother in me made me stubborn enough to keep at you.

"Right now I am crying because I am so happy and proud of you—and of me!"

Education is not the filling of a pail, but the lighting of a fire.

William Butler Yeats

Perhaps the most valuable result of all education is the ability to make yourself do the thing you have to do, when it ought to be done, whether you like it or not; it is the first lesson that ought to be learned, and however early a

*man's training begins, it is probably the last
lesson he learns thoroughly.*

Thomas Huxley

*Education is what survives when what has
been learnt has been forgotten.*

B. F. Skinner

*Education is the ability to listen to almost
anything without losing your temper or your
self-confidence.*

Robert Frost

*The ultimate goal of the educational system is
the shift to the individual the burden of
pursuing his education.*

John W. Gardner

*The test and the use of education is to find
pleasure in the use of the mind.*

*Education today, more than ever before, must
see clearly the dual objectives: education for
living and educating for making a living.*

James Mason Wood

CELEBRATION OF MOTHERS

Often the best lessons that our children learn in their first foray away from home are not those of the classroom.

Good friends of mine whose children or grandchildren have learned much of life in the "outside world" have sent me letters containing humorous anecdotes on lessons learned in university. I would like to share just a few of them with you.

Dear Mom,

Please send me some postage stamps. You have no idea how expensive they are here!

I don't know what Kelly plans to do when she graduates, but judging from her letters home I believe it will be something to do with fundraising.

I was excited when Kevin told me he had learned to divide his washing into three separate loads. Then he told me what they were: terribly dirty, wash for sure; really dirty, but wearable in an emergency; really dirty, wash if you have enough change left after loads 1 and 2.

Cold pizza is good breakfast food.

If you wear your clothes to bed you can sleep ten minutes longer in the morning.

Calling home collect saves lots of money.

You can live for a long time on macaroni and cheese and peanut butter on toast.

Take the giblets out of the turkey before you cook it.

I never knew how much my mother did for me until I had to do it for myself.

A "care package" from home makes everybody in the dorm feel good.

When you come home to visit mom will always send you back to school with the "leftovers." Mom's leftovers are usually a good two weeks' worth of food.

No matter how "cool" you are, your mother is going to hug you when she comes to visit—and you'll love it.

Each of us has our own idea of what "success" is. Often young people feel that success is based on how much you earn or what you own. My mother never attended university, nor did she become wealthy, but she was a success at living, which is the greatest success of all.

I believe these words by Ralph Waldo Emerson best explain "success."

CELEBRATION OF MOTHERS

To laugh often and much; to win respect of intelligent people and the affection of children; to earn the appreciation of honest critics and endure the betrayal of false friends; to appreciate beauty; to find the best in others; to leave the world a bit better, whether by a healthy child, a garden patch or a redeemed social condition; to know even one life has breathed easier because you have lived. This is to have succeeded.

Success is the progressive realization of a worthy ideal.

Earl Nightengale

Of course, there is no formula for success, except, perhaps, an unconditional acceptance of life and what it brings

Arthur Rubenstein

The secret of success is constancy of purpose.

Benjamin Disraeli

Can there be anything more heartbreaking than the death of a child?

Mike went off to university as happy as any young man could possibly be. An outstanding skier, a brilliant student and an all-around fine, popular person. He was excelling in his selected program of science as well as his skiing on the university team.

The ski team was in a bus heading for a weekend of competition in New Hampshire when the driver lost control on glare ice and the bus slid sideways down an embankment, coming to a rest against a tree.

The skiers and their coaches were shaken and bruised, but none seemed to be badly hurt except Mike, who was unconscious and bleeding from a severe laceration to the head.

An ambulance was summoned, and Mike was transported to the nearest hospital. Doctors there quickly determined that Mike was very badly injured and he was subsequently transported, by helicopter, to a bigger and better equipped centre. Mike's parents were called and, in a haze of worry and fear, they raced to be with their son.

On their arrival, the news was not good. Mike had a severely fractured skull and was in a deep coma. He was being kept alive on life support systems and his prognosis was very poor.

Don and Joan were beside themselves with grief. How could this happen to their wonderful son? They walked up and down the hospital corridors hardly able to think or speak.

Later in the evening the doctors spoke with them. "I know that this is a tremendously difficult time for you, but if we are unable to save Michael, would you think about organ donation?"

Throughout the night, Mike's condition continued to deteriorate and it soon became apparent that not even the finest doctors in the world were going to be able to save him.

By now, Mike's brother and sisters had joined their parents at the hospital. In a family conference, they talked about what Mike would have wanted.

"Dad, you know that Mike always said that if something should happen to him, he wanted to donate his organs to others."

And so the family made the most difficult decision that anyone is ever called upon to make.

Mike passed away the next morning, but he was about to change a number of lives forever.

Although the family was heartbroken, they were able to take a small measure of comfort that Mike's passing had given life to others.

We joined hundreds of mourners at Mike's funeral, where we grieved with the family over their devastating loss.

Several days after the funeral, I read a letter in the newspaper that touched me deeply. It could have been written directly to Mike's family. It was a thank-you note from the recipient of a heart transplant, and it read, in part, "I am a heart transplant recipient. Eighteen months after surgery, I am forty-one years old, healthy, happy, and leading a normal life. It is like a miracle. I feel so blessed.

"I owe this life to someone whom I never met, some healthy young person who died unexpectedly. I will be eternally grateful to the family who allowed their loved one's heart to be donated.

"My message is to that unknown family. There is no way that I can adequately thank you. I think of you every day and pray for you every night, and I shall do so for the rest of my life."

Not one of us imagines that we shall die at an early age. How wonderful it is that families such as Mike's give others the gift of life when the lives of their loved ones are tragically cut short.

> *No one may forsake his neighbour when he is in trouble. Everybody is under obligation to help and support his neighbour as he would himself like to be helped.*
>
> *Martin Luther*

The rich and famous are no more immune to misfortune than anyone else.

Barbara Bush and her husband, George, a former president of the United States, also know the tragedy of losing a child.

Robin, their daughter, woke up one morning and announced, "I don't know what to do this morning. I may go out and lie on the grass and watch the cars go by, or I might just stay in bed."

Knowing that this did not sound normal for a three-year-old, Barbara took her to her pediatrician. After doing several tests, the doctors gave the family the diagnosis—leukemia.

George's uncle, Dr. John Walker, was a physician at the famous New York cancer centre, Memorial Sloan-Kettering. He recognized that Robin had very little hope of survival, but felt that they should treat her on the chance that a cancer breakthrough might occur.

Robin began a course of treatment, but the side-effects were devastating and it wasn't long before the little girl slipped into a coma. As her mother put it, "Her death was very peaceful. One minute she was there and the next she was gone."

Barbara and George Bush shared the pain that every family feels on the loss of a child.

In a letter to his mother, George wrote, "But she is still with us. We need her and yet we have her. We can't touch her, and yet we can feel her. We hope she'll stay in our house for a long, long time."

There is a wonderful poem that I think of when I remember friends or family members we have lost.

HIGH FLIGHT

Oh! I have slipped the surly bonds of earth
And danced the skies on laughter-silvered
 wings,
Sunward I've climbed, and joined the tumbling
 mirth
Of sun-split clouds—and done a hundred things
You have not dreamed of—wheeled and soared
 and swung
High in the sunlit silence. Hov'ring there
I've chased the shouting wind along, and flung
My eager craft through footless halls of air.
Up, up the long delirious burning blue,
I've topped the windswept heights with easy
 grace
Where never lark, or even eagle flew—
And, while the silent lifting wind I've trod
The high untrespassed sanctity of space,
Put out my hand and touched the face of God.

John Gillespie McGee, Jr.

Several days of the year bring their own special memories. Christmas, Valentine's Day, Easter, and Thanksgiving are all times for families to share their love and create traditions and memories to last a lifetime.

In our family, these days have given us a chance to come together, share a delicious meal, and enjoy the company of our favourite people, our family members.

On New Year's Day, Marg, Bruce and I, with occasional help from the children and grandchildren, enjoy a time to look back at the year just past.

We take down our appointment calendars, make a pot of tea, bring out the Christmas cookies, and review the year, month by month. The little notes on the calendar, such as "Justin and Jenny's hockey game, 3 p.m." or "Martha's for dinner" are reminders of all the people seen and places visited during the year.

Most of the reminders bring back happy memories. Some, such as "Carl's funeral, 11 a.m.," will bring tears, but even those times are better when shared.

Our "yearly review" usually takes many hours, but they are hours well spent, as we laugh and reminisce and look forward to the year to come.

Memory is the diary that we all carry about with us.

Oscar Wilde

For those of us of the Christian faith, the Easter celebration is the basis of our religion—belief in the life to come after death.

When my husband, George, was alive, Easter was the day of the year that he most enjoyed. It was the day that gave him a great sense of renewal.

On that Friday before Easter, known as Good Friday, my granddaughter Phyllis, her husband Bill, and the twins Justin and Jenny come over to make hot cross buns. It is thought that these small cakes originated in ancient Greece, as offerings to the Olympic gods. They were tiny loaves of bread, spiced and sweetened and marked with a design shaped like an ox's horns. The early Christian Church copied the custom but changed the design to that of a cross.

When I was a little girl, we would go to my grandma's house and she would bring out the old family recipe for these delicious buns. We children would put on our aprons and, with Grandma's help, we would make several dozen of the buns. This, to us, was a large—and delectable—part of the Easter celebration.

As we grew older, we took our own children to our mother's home and they, in turn, brought their children to me.

Phyllis brings her children to Marg's home and I am lucky enough to be included in the festivities.

I can remember, like it was yesterday, how much I loved to help bake the buns at Grandma's house. I believe that Justin and Jenny will hold these same memories as they grow older and I hope that this tradition will pass on down through many more generations.

Family makes your heart feel at home.

My kitchen is a mystical place. It is a place where the sounds and the odours carry meaning that transfers from the past and bridges into the future.

Pearl Bailey

I love my mother's kitchen,
For the family gathers there;
The laughter and the joy we share
Are way beyond compare.

The other rooms in our old house
Hold comfort, peace and rest,
But my mother's homey kitchen
Is the room we all love the best.

I remember these lines, but not the author's name. My thanks to him or her.

Canada has become a country of new and diverse cultures, as immigrants, numbering in the hundreds of thousands, arrive each year to begin new lives.

These new Canadians bring with them their own set of traditions and their own history. This helps us to develop our country's cultural heritage. These traditions, handed down from the past, are an important way that "new" Canadians may remember their roots and the countries of their origins.

My dear friend, Olga, who is of Ukrainian origin, is keeping alive an Easter tradition that is an important part of her family's celebration.

The Easter egg, long thought of as a representation of Jesus' birth, is still a part of the modern festival.

Some of the loveliest of the coloured eggs are called *pysanky*, the elaborately designed and decorated Ukrainian Easter eggs.

Olga makes these delicate treasures each year and is now teaching her grandchildren this painstaking art form.

The process involves the use of melted wax, a *kistka* (or stylus) and many colours of dye. There are various basic symbols that are a part of the design, such as diamonds, representing knowledge; the rose, representing loving and caring; and the fish, representing Christianity.

The eggs, when completed, are spectacularly beautiful, but it takes many hours of difficult (and patient) work.

But as Olga explained to me, "You know, Edna, I am not wealthy, nor do I have many possessions to hand down to my children and my grandchildren. What I can give them is a link to their heritage, and maybe this is the most important gift of all."

I could not agree more.

Time cannot steal the treasure
That we carry in our hearts,
Nor ever dim the shining thoughts
Our cherished past imparts.
And memories of the ones we've loved
Still cast their gentle glow,
To grace our days and light our paths
Wherever we may go.

One must care about a world one will not see.

Bertrand Russell

Tradition does not mean that the living are dead, it means that the dead are living.

Harold Macmillan

Family truly is a blessing that I am thankful for every day, but even more so on Thanksgiving Day. Thanksgiving fills a home with special pleasures.

Although we are widely scattered, nearly all of our family members make a great effort to attend the family get-together.

Thanksgiving time....

A wonderful time of rich golden harvests...of family traditions and closeness shared as loved ones gather near...of beautiful memories that keep yesterday's joys ever-present in our hearts.

One of the nicest Thanksgivings that I can remember was one that George, the girls, and I spent away from home. That may sound strange, but let me explain.

It was November, and George had a conference to attend in New York City. Never having been to New York, the girls and I decided to tag along. The conference itself lasted for three days, so the girls and I had a chance to do some sight-seeing on our own. Our plan was to take the subway to a particular museum of interest, but somehow in the dark of the stations we became confused and lost.

"Let's go outside and see if we can find out where we are," I suggested.

We exited the station and found ourselves in what would be described as a ghetto area. Unsure of what to do, I tried to look around while gathering my wits. Across the street, I noticed a nicely dressed woman enter a building.

"Come along," I instructed the girls. "Follow me."

We crossed the street and went through the doorway where I had last seen the woman. As we entered, the familiar smell of roast turkey wafted from an unseen kitchen.

A pleasant, but rather harried, gentleman greeted us. "Thank heaven! Four more helpers."

It turned out that we were in the neighbourhood "soup kitchen."

It was American Thanksgiving Day and a group of volunteers were working hard to prepare a traditional dinner for the less fortunate.

"We'd love to help," one of the girls said, "but we need to tell Daddy where we are."

As the girls took off their coats I used the pay phone to leave a message of our whereabouts at our hotel desk.

There was a lot to do. The men seemed to be slicing the turkey and mashing the potatoes so I set about making gravy, while the others were filling bowls with cranberry sauce or green beans.

The girls finished setting the tables, and then the doors were opened for our dinner guests, of which there were many. Some came on their own, but many of the guests were whole families—and all were hungry!

As people finished their meals, others arrived to take their places. I'm not certain how long we had been working, but I suddenly looked up from my "endless" gravy pan to see George and about twenty of his colleagues, whom I recognized from the conference, rolling up their sleeves to pitch in and help.

We didn't leave the kitchen until well after ten o'clock that night, and I'm not sure if I have ever been more tired. But, for all of us, it was a true "Thanksgiving," and one that we will not forget.

I think our children can learn a powerful lesson about helping others. Almost every city has people in need and places to go for help. Be it a food bank, a Salvation Army hostel, or a local hospital, all are in need of volunteer help. What better way is there to let children be a part of their community than by doing volunteer work? It takes very little time to make an enormous difference.

Teach us to give and not to count the cost.

St. Ignatius of Loyola

The most vivid memories of Christmases past are usually not of the gifts received or given, but of the spirit of love, the special warmth of

CELEBRATION OF MOTHERS

*Christmas worship, the cherished little habits
of the home.*

Lois Rand

*Christmas is anticipation and discovery,
dazzling lights and brilliant colours. Christmas
is the gentle smile of someone dear...the quiet,
heartwarming traditions. Christmas is home
and family and love.*

Barbara Burrow

Christmas is an excellent opportunity to learn of the joys of giving. I believe that children may be given the responsibility, at a very early age, of selecting gifts appropriate for those who will receive them. My grandson, Marshall, and his wife, Jamie, put this theory to the test with their daughter, Bethany.

The year that Bethany turned five, she was given a number of chores to do each week, for which she was given an allowance (part of which was saved in a piggy bank).

Several weeks before Christmas, the piggy bank was opened and the money was added up. With her mother's help, Beth made a list of the people to whom she was giving gifts, and then they figured out how much she could spend on each gift.

Jamie and Marshall went shopping with Bethany, but they let the little girl make her own selections. She spent much time deliberating over her choices, but seemed pleased with the gifts that she had picked.

As Christmas came closer, Beth was becoming excited, not so much with the thoughts of what Santa was going to bring her, but with the thrill of giving her gifts to the family.

When Christmas Day came, Beth watched with eager anticipation as each of her carefully chosen gifts was opened. As each person "oohed" and "aahed," Beth's delight was evident.

When it was time for bed. Beth gave a contented sigh and said, "That was the best Christmas I ever had."

People say that Christmas today is too commercialized. But I have never found it that way. If you spend money to give people joy, you are not being commercial. It is only when you feel obliged to do something about Christmas that the spirit is spoiled.

Eleanor Roosevelt

There is a beautiful Apache blessing that is being read more and more often at wedding ceremonies of all denominations.

I find it very moving.

Now you will feel no rain,
For each of you will be shelter to each other.
Now you will feel no cold,
For each of you will be warmth to each other.
Now there is no more loneliness for you,
For each of you will be companion to the other.
Now you are two bodies,
But there is only one life before you.
Go now to your dwelling place,
To enter into the days of your togetherness
And may your days be good, and long upon the
  earth.

When you are young and in love, all the world seems beautiful.

It was so very long ago, but it truly seems like yesterday, that George asked me to marry him. I was only nineteen years old at the time, and George was quite nervous about approaching my father to ask for my hand. He needn't have been. My father had married my mother when she was very young and so he had a great understanding for young love.

When George sat down with Dad, he was visibly shaking. My father had just two questions to ask of George.

"Do you love Edna?" To which George replied, "Yes sir, with all my heart."

"Will you take care of her forever, no matter what the circumstances?" To which George answered, "Yes sir, I will do that."

"Then her mother and I give you our blessing and wish you every happiness."

We were married on the first day of June with many family members and friends in attendance. I know that more than a few people felt that we were too young, but happily, we proved them wrong.

George and I had a wonderfully happy life together, and although our time was cut short by George's early passing, he lived up to his commitment to my father. He truly loved me and he took care of me in all circumstances.

The night before we were to be married, my mother gave me a letter. Included in her missive to me was something that my grandmother had given to her before own wedding.

It is entitled "Marriage Advice," from 1886.

Let your love be stronger than your hate or anger.

Learn the wisdom of compromises, for it is better to bend a little than to break.

Believe the best rather than the worst.

People have a way of living up or down to your opinion of them.

CELEBRATION OF MOTHERS

Remember that true friendship is the basis for any lasting relationship. The person you choose to marry is deserving of the courtesies and kindnesses you bestow on your friends.

Pass this advice on to your children and your children's children. This advice will last forever.

Loving relationships are a family's best protection against the challenges of the world.

Bernie Wiebe

It is not enough to love those who are near and dear to us. We must show them that we do so.

Lord Avebury

The most important thing a father can do for his children is to love their mother.

Theodore Martin Hesburgh

Who findeth a wife findeth a good thing.

Proverbs 18:22

Often the difference between a successful marriage and a mediocre one consists of leaving about three or four things each day unsaid.

Harlan Miller

Married couples who love each other tell each other a thousand things without talking.

Chinese proverb

When our firstborn child, Mary, came to tell us that she and John were engaged to be married, and to ask our blessing, I was surprised—not that they were going to be married, but that my own reaction was not what I expected it to be.

When your children are young it seems as if they will be young forever, and that your time together is infinite.

Suddenly, your "baby" announces that she is getting married, and it is as if this time has passed in the blink of an eye.

I wanted more time! I wasn't finished with her yet. I hadn't passed on everything she needed to know. I needed her longer.

Of course I smiled and hugged and kissed them both and exclaimed rapturously over her engagement ring, but inside my head I was screaming "Not yet!"

Later in the evening, as George and I were retiring, I headed for the shower, where I let the water pour over me and wash away the tears that streamed down my face. When I had cried away my sadness, I slipped into my nightgown and into bed.

George headed into the bathroom and I heard the shower running. I also heard strange sounds so I went to investigate. George was in the shower sobbing. "I'm not ready to let her go."

We held each other for a very long time that night.

Marriage is our last, best chance to grow up.

Joseph Baith

Love is patient, love is kind, and is not jealous; love does not brag and is not arrogant, does not act unbecomingly; it does not seek its own, is not provoked, does not take into account a wrong suffered, does not rejoice in unrighteousness, but rejoices with the truth; bears all things, believes all things, hopes all things, endures all things.

Love never fails.

*But now abide faith, hope, love, these three;
but the greatest of these is love.*

> *1 Corinthians 13: 4-8, 13*

*Treasure the love you receive above all. It will
survive long after your gold and good health
have vanished.*

*You have my love…the love that links us. Take
it with you into the world.*

> *Pam Brown, to her daughter*

*Love is a great thing. By itself, it makes
everything that is heavy light, and it smoothes
very rough places.*

Every wedding is special but sometimes circumstances dictate that one is even more unique than another.

One of these was the marriage of my godson, Peter.

Peter lived on a farm on Canada's East Coast. After his father passed away, Peter took over the work and kept the farm running smoothly—not an easy job, because it was a very large farm.

Peter was engaged to be married to Catherine, his high school sweetheart, and the two were looking forward to working together on the farm. Peter's mother, Elizabeth, had moved to a small home in the nearby town and Peter and Catherine often visited for dinner.

One afternoon, Peter was working in the field when something in the harvesting machine that his tractor was pulling seemed to jam. He got off the tractor and went to check. It seemed to be a simple problem to correct, but as he pulled the lever the machine and the tractor jumped backwards, knocking him to the ground and trapping his leg under the machine.

He was in excruciating pain, but he managed to remove his shirt and wave it so as to attract the attention of one of the field hands.

It took some doing but eventually he was freed. They transferred him to a waiting ambulance and rushed to the hospital.

The doctor met with Catherine and Elizabeth, but his news was not good. Peter's leg had been shattered and the doctor felt that amputation was the best answer.

"No," said Elizabeth softly.

"I beg your pardon?" said the doctor.

"I said, No!" Elizabeth protested more strongly. "You may not cut off his leg! If you can't help us we'll go elsewhere but you won't cut off my son's leg!"

The doctor hesitated but something in Elizabeth's determination gave him pause.

"Well I suppose we could try…"

Seven hours later Peter was in an enormous cast, but he still had his leg.

It would be a long and arduous rehabilitation. It was many months before he could stand and many more before he could begin to walk.

A little more than a year after the accident we gathered in the small church to see Peter and Catherine exchange their vows.

As the beautiful couple turned to walk down the aisle the congregation broke into spontaneous applause.

Peter grinned, and turned to his mother and mouthed, "Thank you."

Luctor et Emergo. "I struggle and I come through." The motto of Notre Dame College of Saskatchewan could apply equally to Peter and his mother, Elizabeth.

A happy marriage is a long conversation that seems too short.

André Maurois

The great secret of a successful marriage is to treat all disasters as incidents and none of the incidents as disasters.

Harold Nicolson

CELEBRATION OF MOTHERS

I would like to have engraved inside every wedding band, "Be kind to one another." This is the Golden Rule of marriage and the secret of making love last through the years.

A house is built of logs and stone,
Of tiles and posts and piers;
A home is built of loving deeds
That stands a thousand years.

Victor Hugo

God bless our home and help us to love each
    other true;
To make our home the kind of place where
    everything we do
Is filled with love and kindness,
A dwelling place for thee,
And help us, God, each moment,
To live more helpfully.

You can no more measure a home by inches or weigh it by ounces, than you can set up boundaries of a summer breeze, or calculate the fragrance of a rose. Home is the love which is in it.

Edward Whiting

Home is not where you live, but where they understand you.

Christian Morgenstern

I have come back again to where I belong; not an enchanted place, but the walls are strong.

D. H. Roth

This lovely Welsh blessing hangs in the home of each member of our family. It is an ever-present reminder of the commitment made as we each entered into that wonderful union—marriage.

A house full of sunshine,
Two hearts full of cheer,
Love that grows deeper
Each day of the year.

Our daughter Margaret was also very young when she and Bruce decided to marry. She, of course, had a simple argument, "Well, Mary was younger than I am when *she* got married."

Her father walked her down the aisle on a very warm day in July.

I suppose because Marg was our second child to marry, I was more able to relax and enjoy the wedding. Where I worried about every detail on Mary's day, experience let me know that things, in fact, would go well, and as long as we were organized I needn't become overly tense if we had a few snags along the way.

Indeed, where I was so nervous that I can scarcely recall very much at all about Mary's wedding, Marg's is so clear that I can almost run it like a beautiful movie through my mind.

From the roses and white candles in the church, the pale blue dresses on the bridesmaids, Marg's beautiful hand-embroidered gown, her father's proud smile as he walked her down the aisle, the magnificent rose-covered trellis that was the entrance to the garden reception, the guests all dressed in their finest, to the beautiful music played by a small group of tuxedoed musicians—it is a splendid day in my life that I have enjoyed many times over.

A good marriage is that in which each appoints the other guardian of his solitude. Once the realization is accepted that even between the closest human beings infinite distances continue to exist, a wonderful living side by side can grow up, if they succeed in loving the distance between them which makes it possible for each to see the other whole and against a wide sky.

Rainer Maria Rilke

The strongest foundation for a marriage is friendship.

My son-in-law Bruce, on the occasion of his forty-fifth anniversary, remarked "You know, Mother, Marg and I are very lucky. We've been blessed with wonderful children. Our family unit with parents, aunts, uncles, and cousins is strong and supportive.

"But most important is that Marg and I have developed a wonderful friendship together. Some people may not realize that friendship is the strongest foundation for a marriage."

I'll always be there for you. I hope you know, but you are free—you must grow away.

The mother–child relationship is paradoxical and, in a sense, tragic. It requires the most intense love on the mother's side, yet this very love must help the child grow away from the mother and become fully independent.

Erich Fromm

CELEBRATION OF MOTHERS

My mother wanted me to be her wings, to fly as she never quite had the courage to do. I loved her for that. I love the fact that she wanted to give birth to her own image.

Erica Jong

There comes a time, when the last child has left home, that you suddenly realize that you are only two again.

The house is quiet. Rooms that once looked as if a hurricane had struck now stay too neat from day to day and week to week. The housework that you thought would never end, has.

The phone that once rang endlessly at any hour of the day now sits quiet, a testament to the loss of happy chatter and plans made, changed, and made again.

The "birds" have flown and the "nest" is empty.

Some mothers find this change difficult to deal with. The busy world that we lived in has disappeared and another, more settled and quiet, has taken its place.

For some it becomes a time of mourning—for others it is a glorious gift, a time to find "us" again.

I was very lucky. My husband made the transition very easy for me.

"Edna, you have always wanted to write. Let's make a studio for you. We can go off to some antique shops and get a desk and some shelves for your books. We'll get a comfortable chair and you can begin at once to put those brilliant words on paper. This is such a wonderful and exciting time. I am so happy for both of us!"

This is the true joy in life, the being used for a purpose recognized by yourself as a mighty one....

George Bernard Shaw

When one door of happiness closes, another opens; but often we look so long at the closed doors that we do not see the one which has been opened for us.

Helen Keller

You are the gate through which it comes into the world, and you will be allowed to have charge of it for a period; after that, it will leave you and blossom out into its own free life—and there it is, for you to watch, living its life in freedom.

Agatha Christie

CELEBRATION OF MOTHERS

Our lives do not cease to be important because our children have left home. Remember, you are needed. There is at least one important work to be done that will not be done without you to do it.

You can not teach a child to take care of himself unless you will let him try to take care of himself. He will make mistakes; and out of these mistakes will come his wisdom.

Henry Ward Beecher

Mothers can get weaned as well as babies.

T. C. Haliburton

"You are a grandmother!"

Perhaps the sweetest words in the English language, they are also the most surprising.

Wasn't it just last week that I had my own babies? How could I possibly be a grandmother?

And my handsome young husband—how is it possible that he is a grandfather?

As we walked down the corridor of the hospital toward the nursery, I held on very tightly to George's hand and there were butterflies in my stomach.

We arrived at the window and gazed upon the dozens of newborns in their cribs. George held up the name card, and the nurse reached in to lift the tiny bundle that was our grandchild.

She brought him to the window and suddenly we were looking at the child of our child. George and I began a miracle and a miracle continues.

He was incredibly beautiful: little round cheeks, long lashes, brown peach fuzz hair—there never was a baby as perfect.

I wanted to stand there and look at him for hours—I never wanted to leave that window. The nurse put him back but I continued to stare...child of my child.

A miracle.

If your baby is beautiful and perfect, never cries or fusses, sleeps on schedule and burps on demand, an angel all the time—you're the grandmother.

Teresa Bloomingdale

The joy of becoming a mother was a prelude to the joy of becoming a grandmother.

Vera Allen-Smith

If I'd known grandchildren were going to be so much fun, I'd have had them first.

When you become a grandmother, you need a larger purse to hold all the photos of the grandchildren.

Becoming a grandmother is really quite strange. There is your baby sitting with a baby of her own in her arms.

When grandparents get together, you can be sure that the conversation will turn, quite often, to the grandchildren.

My friends, Will and Muriel, are proud grandparents who regularly enjoy the company of their grandchildren in their home. Whenever they stop by to see me, they have stories to tell.

"You know, Edna, Will has come up with a terrific way to entertain the grandkids when they visit. Some months ago, we bought a new mattress and box spring, but Will, ever the pack rat, saved the old set.

"Now, when the little ones come over, Will gets out the 'trampoline' and they are happy for hours.

"One of the great joys of being a grandparent is that we are given a chance to enjoy the company of the grandchildren, and just when they begin to get tired and cranky, Mom and Dad take them away, leaving you with the precious memories."

It was Grandpa's turn to give little Joey his bath.

As he popped him into the tub, he said "Well Joey, I bet we did that faster than Grandma usually does it didn't we?"

"Yes Grandpa, we did, but Grandma usually takes off my socks and shoes first."

My good friend Emily is a "foster grandparent," a volunteer who works with children who have been deprived of a normal childhood. Several years ago, Emily and I spent a day visiting with her foster granddaughter. What a delightful child she was.

Emily explained to me that Jessica was a very quiet and troubled little girl when she first met her, about one year previously. She had come from a broken home, where she had been an unwanted child. Without the stimulation normally given to children, she soon fell behind her peers and, when she started school, she simply couldn't cope. She became more withdrawn until she would no longer speak at all.

What a difference a year of loving and caring has made in Jessica's life. It took a great deal of patience for Emily to continue to read or talk to this little girl when she reacted as a statue for months. Her love and patience paid off, however, and a breakthrough came when Jessica asked Emily to read Cinderella to her again. From that day on, Jessica seemed to realize that Emily was someone who loved and cared about her.

Although it will take a very long time for Jessica to overcome her earlier deprivation, her lively chatter gives hope that she could become a happy, well-adjusted person. It gives Emily great satisfaction to help this little girl blossom.

You have no grandchildren yet? A foster grandparenting program could be a marvellous way to begin.

Our grandchildren accept us for ourselves, without rebuke or effort to change us, as no one in our entire lives has ever done—not our parents, siblings, spouses, friends and, hardly ever, our grown children.

Ruth Goode

To our grandchildren, what we tell them about their parents' childhood and our own young years is living history.

Grandmothers don't have to do anything except be there.

Patsy Gray

THE HERITAGE BOOK

The bond between child and grandparent can, indeed, be the purest, least complicated form of human love.

Foster W. Cline

A wonderful way to see the family from generation to generation is with old photos, home movies, and now with videos.

When my great-granddaughter Bethany, the youngest member of our family, celebrated her first birthday we enjoyed a large get-together at Marshall and Jamie's home to share the occasion.

Her grandparents gave a gift to Beth through her parents. They presented Marshall and Jamie with a small portable video recorder with lots of cassettes for filming important events in Bethany's life.

"The gift of her childhood for her to see," was how they worded the card.

Since then, Marshall has recorded birthday parties, gymnastics meets, first days of school, and many other special events. As she grows older Beth will be able to look back on her childhood—but even more important, she will be able to share the significant happenings of her life with her children and grandchildren.

CELEBRATION OF MOTHERS

Grandparents should be one of a child's most valuable resources. They should be gentle teachers of the way life was and the way it should be.

John Rosemond

A grandmother is a little girl who suddenly shows up one day with a touch of grey in her hair.

Grandchildren are the dots that connect the lines from generation to generation.

Lois Wyse

Grandchildren are a renewal of life, a little bit of us going into the future.

Just about the time a woman thinks her work is done, she becomes a grandmother.

Edward H. Dreschnack

In the years since I began following the ways of my grandmothers I have come to value the teachings, stories and daily examples of living which they shared with me. I pity the younger girls of the future who will miss out on meeting some of these fine old women.

B. H. Wolf

Give your grandchildren a gift they are sure to appreciate—your undivided attention.

My "Poppa" died before my three girls were born. My grandfather and I shared a very close relationship and while I missed him dearly, I was even more saddened by the thought that my children would never know this wise, gentle man.

After Poppa passed away, Grammie moved in with my parents. She enjoyed being with them but she valued her privacy and would often retreat to her room and shut the door. Under no circumstances was anyone to bother her when the door was closed.

Whenever I would take the girls for a visit they were reminded of the closed-door rule.

"You must wait until Grammie opens her door and then you may visit with her," I would say each time.

It was quite a sight to see the three little ones sitting on the floor in the hall staring at the closed door. I think they believed that they could wish the door open if they tried hard enough.

Eventually, however, Grammie would open the door and the girls would be invited in to visit. It was during these visits that the girls got to know Poppa.

"Did you know that Poppa liked to carve wood? He made the cribbage board in Grammie's room."

"Did you know that Poppa could write poems? Grammie read some of them to us today."

"Did you know that Poppa's favourite food was chocolate cake? He liked Grammie's cake the best of any and she's going to show us how to make it."

"Poppa didn't have a pet when he was little. That's why they had nine cats when our grandma was a little girl."

"Poppa loved gardening."

"Poppa was just like us. He didn't like brussels sprouts."

Each time that we visited the girls came to know a little more about Poppa. Grammie would open the scrap books filled with pictures so that the girls could see him as well.

Although they never met Poppa, Grammie made sure that my girls knew the man that I had so cherished.

Grandmothers hold in their heads a world you never knew. Now they are giving it to you to store with your own memories—to be handed down to your grandchildren in turn.

Pam Brown

A friend of mine had her young grandson stay overnight. He had been playing outside, so by bedtime he needed a bath. After bathing him she put on some nice smelling powder, got him into his pyjamas, combed his hair, and tucked him into his bed with clean fresh sheets.

As she settled in beside him to read him a story he looked up and remarked "Gee Grandma, you would make a nice mother."

If nothing is going well, call your grandmother.

        Italian proverb

The true accolade was not only my father saying he would be proud of me, but that my grandmother would have been proud of me.

        William H. Hastie

Grandma always made you feel she had been waiting to see you all day and now the day was complete.

        M. DeMaree

Did you think that being a grandparent was easy? There is a professor in the United States who is teaching a course called "Becoming a Better Grandparent." He feels that many of today's grandparents should go back to school to learn how to relate to their grandchildren.

Says Professor Strom, of Arizona State University, "The number one objective of being an effective grandparent is to become a valuable and positive role model for your grandchildren to look up to."

I pass along a few of the professor's tips for better grandparenting.

Try to think like a kid. You have to know what it's like to be a youngster today. Children face a multitude of problems that didn't exist when you were young.

Think like a parent. It is important to know what your grown children are going through.

Develop a one-to-one relationship. Too often grandparents see their grandchildren as a group. It is important to spend time with each of your grandchildren individually.

Continue to learn. Keep up with new developments. Stay current or risk becoming obsolete to your grandchildren.

Confide in your grandchildren. It is important to discuss personal thoughts and beliefs. If you confide in them, they'll confide in you.

Spend your free time wisely. Be a positive role model. When you show your grandchildren that volunteering to work for charities is important to you it will be important to them also.

Don't spoil kids with money. Instead of giving a kid a new disc player give them a savings bond or money put in a college fund.

Even if your grandchild lives too far away to visit often, keep up the relationship with phone calls and letters.

Love your grandchildren unconditionally.

There's nothing like having grandchildren to restore your faith in heredity.

Doug Larsen

A grandmother is a combination of work-worn hands after a lifetime of toil, a loving heart, and endless stories of the days when her family was young.

Elizabeth Faye

I would like to end this little book with a letter of thanks.

We all do the best that we can while we are bringing up our children. Sometimes it can be difficult.

Good friends of mine went through a challenging period in their lives. A business failed and they lost their home and savings, all while their four children were in university. Both parents took on two jobs and with courage and hard work managed to keep the children in school until graduation.

One of their daughters wrote a thank-you note after her graduation. It is a note that could be written to any mother in the world—a thank-you that shows true understanding of the role of "Mother."

Hi Mom!

Happy Mother's Day! Happy Birthday! I'm sorry I won't be there to celebrate with you. Now that I'm off in the real world and realize how much I miss you, I also realize how lucky I am.

I really want to thank you for everything. Thank you for always knowing best. You not only taught me well, you have always been the perfect role model for me—handling work, the house, four kids—you always found time for us. Thank you for always making my games, meets, and races, and always being the loudest to cheer from the crowd. Thank you for driving to the ends of the earth to get us there on time. Thank you for always being interested in my life. Thank you for making me do my home work—for making me see why it was so important to do well in school. Thank you for letting me go ahead and make my own decisions even if you knew they weren't always right.

Thank you for all of the travelling that we did, realizing how much there was to see.

Thank you for teaching me right and wrong and always knowing what the right thing was.

Thank you for telling me to get my elbows off the table.

Thank you for being so strong—for making it through the toughest times and coming out on top.

Thank you for teaching me what things in life just aren't worth worrying about and that money isn't everything.

Thank you for my wonderful brother and sisters, and for teaching us the importance of family. Thank you for providing my education, even when you could not afford it.

CELEBRATION OF MOTHERS

*Thank you for all of the sacrifices you made,
and know that I would make them for you too.*

*Thank you for always being you. You are the
best thing that could have happened to me. I'm
sorry if I never took the time to thank you
earlier.*

I love you,

Christy.